How To Use This Study Guide

This 15-lesson study guide corresponds to *"Ten Thing To Make Your Life Strong" With Rick Renner* (**Renner TV**). Each lesson in this study guide covers a topic that is addressed during the program series, with questions and references supplied to draw you deeper into your own private study of the Scriptures on this subject.

To derive the most benefit from this study guide, consider the following:

First, watch or listen to the program prior to working through the corresponding lesson in this guide. (Programs can also be viewed at **renner.org** by clicking on the Media/Archives links or on our Renner Ministries YouTube channel.)

Second, take the time to look up the scriptures included in each lesson. Prayerfully consider their application to your own life.

Third, use a journal or notebook to make note of your answers to each lesson's Study Questions and Practical Application challenges.

Fourth, invest specific time in prayer and in the Word of God to consult with the Holy Spirit. Write down the scriptures or insights He reveals to you.

Finally, take action! Whatever the Lord tells you to do according to His Word, do it.

For added insights on this subject, it is recommended that you obtain Rick Renner's book *Sparkling Gems From the Greek, Volumes 1* and *2*. You may also select from Rick's other available resources by placing your order at **renner.org** or by calling 1-800-742-5593.

LESSON 1

TOPIC
A Passion for Souls — Part 1

SCRIPTURES
1. **Matthew 28:19, 20** — Go ye therefore, and teach all nations, baptizing them in the name of the Father, and of the Son, and of the Holy Ghost: Teaching them to observe all things whatsoever I have commanded you: and, lo, I am with you always, even unto the end of the world.
2. **Romans 1:16** — For I am not ashamed of the gospel of Christ: for it is the power of God unto salvation to every one that believeth....
3. **Ezekiel 3:18, 19 (*NKJV*)** — When I say to the wicked, "You shall surely die" and you give him no warning, nor speak to warn the wicked from his wicked way, to save his life, that same wicked man shall die in his iniquity; but his blood I will require at your hand. Yet, if you warn the wicked, and he does not turn from his wickedness, nor from his wicked way, he shall die in his iniquity; but you have delivered your soul.

GREEK WORDS
1. "ashamed" — ἐπαισχύνομαι (*epaischunomai*): to be shamed, disgraced, embarrassed, red-faced
2. "power" — δύναμις (*dunamis*): the full force of an army
3. "salvation" — σῴζω (*sodzo*): salvation; deliverance on every level

SYNOPSIS
Walking through the Novodevichy Cemetery in Moscow is like walking through volumes of Russian history. The remains of renowned scientists, generals, politicians, artists, composers, and musicians are all interred in this sacred space. Name after famous name of legendary people from Russia and the entire former USSR are memorialized in statues and in markers of bronze and granite. It is truly an amazing sight to see.

A Note From Rick Renner

I am on a personal quest to see a "revival of the Bible" so people can establish their lives on a firm foundation that will stand strong and endure the test as the end-time storm winds begin to intensify.

In order to experience a revival of the Bible in your personal life, it is important to take time each day to read, receive, and apply its truths to your life. James tells us that if we will continue in the perfect law of liberty — refusing to be forgetful hearers but determined to be doers — we will be blessed in our ways. As you watch or listen to the programs in this series and work through this corresponding study guide, I trust that you will search the Scriptures and allow the Holy Spirit to help you hear something new from God's Word that applies specifically to your life. I encourage you to be a doer of the Word that He reveals to you. Whatever the cost, I assure you — it will be worth it.

> Thy words were found, and I did eat them;
> and thy word was unto me the joy and rejoicing of mine heart:
> for I am called by thy name, O Lord God of hosts.
> — Jeremiah 15:16

Your brother and friend in Jesus Christ,

Rick Renner

Rick Renner

Unless otherwise indicated, all scripture quotations are taken from the *King James Version* of the Bible.

Scripture quotations marked (*AMPC*) are taken from the *Amplified® Bible, Classic Edition*. Copyright © 1954, 1958, 1962, 1964, 1965, 1987 by The Lockman Foundation. Used by permission. **www.Lockman.org**.

Scripture quotations marked (*NKJV*) are taken from the *New King James Version*®. Copyright © 1982 by Thomas Nelson. Used by permission. All rights reserved.

Scripture quotations marked (*NLT*) are taken from the Holy Bible, *New Living Translation*, copyright © 1996, 2004, 2015 by Tyndale House Foundation. Used by permission of Tyndale House Publishers, Inc., Carol Stream, Illinois 60188. All rights reserved.

Scripture quotations marked (*TLB*) are taken from *The Living Bible* copyright © 1971. Used by permission of Tyndale House Publishers, Inc., Carol Stream, Illinois 60188. All rights reserved.

Ten Things To Make Your Life Strong

Copyright © 2019 by Rick Renner
1814 W. Tacoma St.
Broken Arrow, OK 74012-1406

Published by Rick Renner Ministries
www.renner.org

ISBN 13: 978-1-6803-1626-1

ISBN 13 eBook: 978-1-6803-1664-3

All rights reserved. No portion of this book may be reproduced, stored in a retrieval system, or transmitted in any form or by any means — electronic, mechanical, photocopy, recording, scanning, or other — except for brief quotations in critical reviews or articles, without the prior written permission of the Publisher.

Where are these people today? We know their physical remains are in the ground, but where have their souls and spirits gone? The Bible teaches we will *all* go to one of two places after we pass from this earth: *Heaven* or *hell*. If we truly love people — and if we truly care about our family members and friends — we will do all we can to share the truth of the Gospel so we can rescue those who are perishing without Christ from certain destruction.

The 15 lessons in this study *Ten Things To Make Your Life Strong* will focus on the following topics:

- A Passion for Souls
- A Passion for God's Word
- A Passion for the Holy Spirit
- A Passion for Worship
- A Passion for Prayer
- A Passion for Giving
- A Passion for Holiness
- A Passion for Humility
- A Passion for Authority
- A Passion for the Fear of the Lord

The emphasis of this lesson:

In order to live as strong Christians, we must possess a passion for souls. Everyone living is an eternal being with a spirit that will spend eternity either in Heaven or in hell. God has given us the responsibility to share the truth — warning people of the consequences of rejecting Christ and entering eternity with an unregenerate spirit — and then to encourage them with the Good News of salvation through the Savior Jesus Christ.

The Great Commission — Because There's Life Beyond the Grave!

There *is* life beyond the grave. Jesus knew and taught this regularly. He had a passion for souls and gave His very life to save all who would believe on Him as the *only* Way, Truth, and Life (*see* John 14:6). After His resurrection from the dead, before being taken back up to Heaven, Jesus gave us His Great Commission.

> Go ye therefore, and teach all nations, baptizing them in the name of the Father, and of the Son, and of the Holy Ghost: Teaching them to observe all things whatsoever I have commanded you: and, lo, I am with you always, even unto the end of the world.
>
> — Matthew 28:19, 20

The word "go" in this verse in the original Greek would better be translated, "Go, and be *constantly* going." This "going" is to be a lifestyle or habit. In other words, Jesus was not describing a short-term mission trip or sporadic church visitation or organized outreached. He was describing a commitment for reaching souls that is so passionate that you keep going and *continually* going, ready and willing at all times to share the truth with whomever God brings across your path.

What Jesus gave us was a commandment, not a suggestion. We are to go *and keep going* to reach people who have never heard the Gospel. If we're going to be obedient to Him and His command, we must be committed to go and keep going in order to reach the lost. Wherever the Gospel is being shared, the power of God is in operation. Where it is not shared, the power of God is not in operation.

A Promise of Presence and Power

In our "going," we are to be about the business of "…baptizing them in the name of the Father, and of the Son, and of the Holy Ghost…." (Matthew 28:19). This is to "all nations." We are not called to try to affect a few people in every nation. We are called to affect entire nations for Christ, baptizing and making them disciples through the preaching and teaching — the proclaiming — of God's Word.

Then Jesus made this promise: "…And, lo, I am with you always, even unto the end of the world" (Matthew 28:20). This little word "lo" could be translated, *And, wow!* This word was used to express a person's sense of amazement about something. Here, it emphasizes Jesus' amazement at what He was about to promise. By saying, "And, lo…," it was as if He was saying, "*Wow — this is amazing!* If you go and do what I've just said — will I ever be with you, even unto the end of the world!"

This is a promise of Christ's presence and power for those who "go." It is not a promise for everyone; rather, it's a commitment by Jesus Himself toward those who obey His instruction. If you will go *and keep going* into all the world — habitually reaching the lost and having a passion for souls — Jesus said, "Wow! Will I ever be with you!" It is His personal promise of divine power to you and to *everyone* who passionately attempts to reach the lost. That is what we read in the Great Commission in Matthew 28:19 and 20.

The Early Church Had a Passion for Souls

The Early Church believed in and obeyed Jesus' Great Commission. They literally went into the whole world with the message of Jesus Christ. From the beginning of the book of Acts to the end, the Bible tells us of believers who shared Christ with others, and the results were always miraculous. The power of God consistently showed up to accompany the preaching of the Gospel.

As a result, the Early Church supernaturally grew. They literally exploded with divine power. Acts 2:47 says that the Lord added to their numbers daily. They began to supernaturally grow because they were *continually going*. Their lives had been changed by Christ, and they were eager and not ashamed to speak about Him to other people.

This was the promise of Jesus: "If you go, *wow* — will I ever be with you!" Likewise, when *we* go, Jesus promised that He will ever be with *us*! It was and is a promise of His divine power. Nothing brings the power of God to the Church like sharing Christ! In fact, this act of obedience is the game-changer when it comes to ministry to others.

When You Release the Gospel, You Release *Power*

Releasing the Gospel releases God's power. This is why the apostle Paul said, "For I am not ashamed of the gospel of Christ: for it is the power of God unto salvation to every one that believeth…" (Romans 1:16).

The word "ashamed" in this verse comes from the Greek word *epaischunomai*, which means *to be shamed, disgraced, embarrassed, or red-faced*. By using this word, Paul was saying, "My face is not red with embarrassment. I'm not ashamed, and I feel no disgrace whatsoever regarding the Gospel." Paul felt no shame because he had experienced the power of God himself, and he experienced it in his ministry to others as the Gospel was shared.

The word "power" is the Greek word *dunamis*. It is an old Greek word that describes *the advancing power of an entire army*. This indicates that when you share the Gospel, dynamic power is released. Like a powerful, mighty army, the power of God suddenly appears on the scene, ready to move into action. It is the power of God that brings salvation.

The word "salvation" is the Greek word *sodzo*, which means *salvation or deliverance on every level*. Think about it. Whenever and wherever the Gospel is preached or shared, it brings life-transforming deliverance, healing, and preservation to everyone who believes, which in the Greek actually means *"to the one who is believing."*

Therefore, as we "go and keep on going" in sharing the Good News, the power (*dunamis*) of God will be released. We have Christ's word on it! The Early Church experienced this firsthand. Signs and wonders were a regular occurrence for those early believers.

What Keeps Believers From Sharing the Gospel Today?

Since the Gospel obviously packs such power, why aren't believers sharing the Good News more often? Why are we embarrassed? Why are we ashamed? Why are we "red-faced" about the message of Jesus' saving grace?

First, many people don't feel equipped or trained to do it. Second, some people are afraid of how others will respond. The fear of being ridiculed, looked down upon, or rejected by their peers often paralyzes people into silence.

A third reason for not sharing the Gospel is not having experienced the Baptism in the Holy Spirit. According to Acts 1:8, when a person receives the Baptism in the Holy Spirit, he or she receives power to be a witness for Christ.

If you have not experienced the supernatural infilling of God's Spirit that comes with the baptism in the Holy Spirit, you can receive it today! You can call our office at 1-800-742-5593, and we will pray with you to receive this powerful gift for witnessing about Christ and for living an effective Christian life.

Hell Is a Real Place

As we learned at the opening of this lesson, people are eternal, spiritual beings, and we are all going to spend eternity somewhere. The Bible gives only two options: *Heaven* or *hell*. Interestingly, statistics show that more people believe in the reality of Heaven than the reality of hell. Sadly, this includes many Christians.

The fact is, every one of us is born with a sin nature, and we need to be saved. We cannot save ourselves, which is why Jesus came and lived a sinless life, died on the Cross to redeem us and bring us back to God, and then rose again. Those who do not accept the free gift of salvation through Christ are headed to hell. As harsh and unappealing as that may sound, it is biblical fact (*see* John 3:16-18).

One key indicator that a believer is strong is that he or she loves people enough to share the Gospel with them. Regrettably, many Christians don't really believe hell is a real place, and therefore, they have no urgent motivation to speak the truth. Although they may believe in hell doctrinally or on paper, it remains as merely a theorized element of their creed.

The truth is, if you believe what Jesus said on multiple occasions — that hell *is indeed* a real place — you *will* take action. Instead of passing the days simply talking about the weather and sports, you will prepare yourself and look for opportunities to share the Gospel with your unsaved family members, friends, and others you come in contact with in life.

Once a person breathes his last breath here, he will slip into eternity, and there is nothing that can be done about his eternal destination after that point. The person who dies in his sin, having neither repented nor invited Jesus into his life, will spend eternity in hell. There is no retraction, no second chances, no way to fix things. It's over and his fate is sealed.

As believers, we need a real revelation of hell. Having a glimpse of the reality of hell will help provide a healthy motivation to shake off apathy and get us out of our comfort zone to tell the lost around us about the saving grace of Jesus Christ.

If a Christian has a revelation of hell, but does nothing about it, it reveals one of two things. That Christian either doesn't *really* believe it's the truth, or he lacks the compassionate love of Christ. To know hell is a real place and do nothing to warn the unsaved is unthinkable! But there is hope.

May the Lord break our hearts for the lost as His heart is broken for them.

We Are Called To Warn Others

Through the prophet Ezekiel, God plainly gives us this warning: "When I say to the wicked, 'You shall surely die' and you give him no warning, nor speak to warn the wicked from his wicked way, to save his life, that same wicked man shall die in his iniquity; but his blood I will require at your hand. Yet, if you warn the wicked, and he does not turn from his wickedness, nor from his wicked way, he shall die in his iniquity; but you have delivered your soul" (Ezekiel 3:18, 19 *NKJV*).

If we choose not to share the Gospel with someone who is unsaved that God places in our lives, He will hold us accountable for not telling him how to be saved from eternity in hell. However, if we do share the truth with that person, and he chooses to reject it, we have fulfilled our responsibility.

The Early Church had a firm belief in the reality of hell and acted accordingly. They traveled far and wide, warning people of the dangers of hell and encouraging them with the Good News of salvation through faith in Jesus Christ. They had a passion to reach souls, and so must we today.

STUDY QUESTIONS

> **Study to shew thyself approved unto God, a workman that needeth not to be ashamed, rightly dividing the word of truth.**
> **— 2 Timothy 2:15**

1. In the Great Commission, Jesus instructed us to "Go and make disciples of all nations, baptizing them in the name of the Father and the Son and the Holy Spirit. Teach these new disciples to obey all the commands I have given you..." (Matthew 28:19, 20 *NLT*). What would you say is the difference between *evangelizing* and *making disciples*? Why are both equally important in the Body of Christ? (Consider Ephesians 4:11-16 and 2 Timothy 3:16, 17.)

2. What is Jesus' personal promise to you regarding soul-winning in Matthew 4:19 (also consider Matthew 11:28-30)? According to Proverbs 11:30, sharing the Gospel makes you what? And what does God declare about your evangelistic efforts in Daniel 12:3?

PRACTICAL APPLICATION

But be ye doers of the word, and not hearers only, deceiving your own selves.
—James 1:22

1. If you are not alive when Christ returns to rapture, or "catch away" the Church (*see* 1 Thessalonians 4:17), you will pass from this life by way of the grave. Like the men and women in that Moscow cemetery, a tombstone will mark your final resting place. What do you think *others* would write as your epitaph? What do you think *Jesus* would write as your epitaph? What would *you* want this memorial to say?

2. Jesus promised that His amazing Holy Spirit would empower us to be His witnesses (*see* Acts 1:8). If you have experienced the baptism in the Holy Spirit, what do you love most about it? What has His presence and power specifically enabled you to *say* and *do* that you couldn't have done otherwise? If you have not experienced the baptism in the Holy Spirit but would like to, we would love to pray with you! Please call us at 1-800-742-5593 any weekday 8:00 a.m.-5:00 p.m. CT, and one of our team members will be honored to pray with you.

LESSON 2

TOPIC

A Passion for Souls — Part 2

SCRIPTURES

1. **Matthew 28:19, 20** — Go ye therefore, and teach all nations, baptizing them in the name of the Father, and of the Son, and of the Holy Ghost: Teaching them to observe all things whatsoever I have commanded you: and, lo, I am with you always, even unto the end of the world.

2. **Ezekiel 3:18, 19 (*NKJV*)** — When I say to the wicked, "You shall surely die" and you give him no warning, nor speak to warn the wicked from his wicked way, to save his life, that same wicked man shall die in his iniquity; but his blood I will require at your hand. Yet, if you warn the wicked, and he does not turn from his wickedness, nor

from his wicked way, he shall die in his iniquity; but you have delivered your soul.
3. **Romans 6:23** — For the wages of sin is death; but the gift of God is eternal life through Jesus Christ our Lord.
4. **Matthew 7:14** — Because strait is the gate, and narrow is the way, which leadeth unto life, and few there be that find it.
5. **Revelation 21:8** — But the fearful, and unbelieving, and the abominable, and murderers, and whoremongers, and sorcerers, and idolaters, and all liars, shall have their part in the lake which burneth with fire and brimstone: which is the second death.
6. **James 2:18** — A man may say, Thou hast faith, and I have works: shew me thy faith without thy works, and I will shew thee my faith by my works.

GREEK WORDS

1. "ashamed" — ἐπαισχύνομαι (*epaischunomai*): to be shamed, disgraced, embarrassed, red-faced
2. "power" — δύναμις (*dunamis*): the full force of an army
3. "salvation" — σώζω (*sodzo*): salvation; deliverance on every level

SYNOPSIS

The Novodevichy Cemetery, located in Moscow, is an amazing graveyard marking the final resting place of many remarkable people who once lived and served in Russia and throughout the former Soviet Union. The statues, the monuments, and the tombs themselves serve as a lasting legacy to preserve the memory of these historic individuals.

Yet as one walks among the headstones, he might quietly question, *Where are these people now? Their graves are here and are beautifully kept, but where are their souls and spirits? Where are they spending eternity?*

When people die, they go *somewhere*. The Bible teaches that they go to one of two places: If they die *in Christ*, they go to Heaven to be with Him; if they die in their sin, they pay the ultimate penalty in hell for rejecting Christ.

Eternity is real and it is forever. Jesus Christ died for men's and women's souls because the souls of mankind needed to be saved. He had a dying passion to see the lost saved, and so should we.

The emphasis of this lesson:
To be strong believers, we must have a passion for souls. Jesus had such a passion, and so should we. The Bible is clear that *hell is a real place*. We have a responsibility to do everything we can to share the Gospel so people can hear it, believe, call upon Christ's name, and be saved from going to that awful place.

More than 2,000 years ago, Jesus gave us the Great Commission. Although much time has passed, His words are just as urgent now as they were then, if not more so. He said, "Go ye therefore, and teach all nations, baptizing them in the name of the Father, and of the Son, and of the Holy Ghost: Teaching them to observe all things whatsoever I have commanded you: and, lo, I am with you always, even unto the end of the world" (Matthew 28:19, 20).

As we learned in our last lesson, the phrase "Go ye therefore" in the Greek literally means to *go and keep on going*. In other words, Jesus was not suggesting that we just go on a single mission trip or to occasionally be a part of the home-visitation or evangelism team at your church. He was advocating that we develop a lifestyle of *commitment* to telling others the Good News of salvation through Him.

If we will "go and keep on going," telling others about Jesus, He will fulfill His promise to us in verse 20. He said, "...And, lo, I am with you always, even unto the end of the world." This word "lo" could better be translated from the Greek, *"And wow!"* It's an exclamatory remark. Jesus was so impressed with what He was about to promise us that He stopped and said, "And, *wow* — will I ever be with you, even to the end of the world!"

Evangelism Ignites God's Power

The book of Acts confirms that when God's people shared the Gospel, God's power was released. Their consistent passion to see souls saved ignited His power in remarkable ways. The same opportunity holds true for you. When you open your mouth and begin to sincerely share the Gospel with an unsaved family member, friend, or coworker, Heaven's power will be released on the scene.

Historically, the greatest signs and wonders in the Church came when the Gospel was being preached in a territory for the very first time. Signs and wonders *exploded* on the scene. The power of God came on the scene when and where the Gospel was shared. And the same is true today.

Many believers today talk a lot about the power of God, but we don't see the power of God to the same degree because we're not reaching out to the lost. Remember, God doesn't want us to be "ashamed of the gospel of Christ: for it is the *power* of God unto salvation to every one that believeth…" (Romans 1:16).

People desperately need to hear the simple message of the Gospel, and you and I have the opportunity and responsibility to bring it to them.

Only Two Eternal Options

Romans 6:23 clearly states, "For the wages of sin is death; but the gift of God is eternal life through Jesus Christ our Lord." There are two eternal options that exist before every human being: One is eternal death, and one is eternal life. There is no gray area. What a person chooses to do with Jesus determines the outcome. He can accept God's free gift of salvation through Jesus and receive eternal life — or reject Christ's free gift and pay the wages for sin in eternal death.

Just take a look around you. Every person you see is going somewhere when he or she dies! The person in the cubicle next to you at work, the elderly woman on your street, the cashier at the store, and each of your family members all have a destiny in eternity. They will either die in their sin or they will die in Christ. Those who die *in Christ* will spend eternity with Him in Heaven. Those who die in their sin will spend eternity in hell.

There are *only two options*.

Everyone is born once, but not everyone is born twice. Those who die at a certain age who have only been born once — experiencing only the natural, physical birth — will go to hell. But those who are born twice — experiencing physical birth *and* the supernatural birth of the Spirit of God (*see* John 3:1-18) — will go to Heaven. This is the plain, sobering truth of God's Word, and there is no getting around it.

Jesus said in Matthew 7:14, "Strait is the gate, and narrow is the way, which leadeth unto life, and few there be that find it." In other words, few people are going to Heaven; many are on their way to hell. Jesus died to save people from going there. He warned again and again of its reality, and so must we.

Jesus Taught Regularly About Hell

Regrettably, many Christians today do not really believe in hell. Yes, intellectually, they might agree that such a place exists. But it is more a theory to them than reality. But Jesus had a revelation of hell. Consequently, He taught on the subject of hell three times more than on the subject of Heaven. There is no one in all of history who has a more authoritative voice on the topic of hell than Jesus.

Christ taught about hell so often that His disciples learned about it, believed in it, and passed it on to the Early Church. This is a major reason the First Century believers were so passionate about reaching people with the saving message of Jesus Christ. There was a sense of urgency to do everything within their power to prevent people from going there. We need this same urgency today.

God soberly warns us in Ezekiel 3:18 and 19, "When I say to the wicked, 'You shall surely die' and you give him no warning, nor speak to warn the wicked from his wicked way, to save his life, that same wicked man shall die in his iniquity; but his blood I will require at your hand. Yet, if you warn the wicked, and he does not turn from his wickedness, nor from his wicked way, he shall die in his iniquity; but you have delivered your soul."

If we choose not to share the Gospel with the lost people God places in our life, He will hold us accountable for not telling them the news that can save them from an eternal destiny in hell. But if we do share the truth of salvation through Christ and they reject it, the responsibility rests with them. This may sound strong, but that is exactly what the Bible says.

Jesus had a revelation of hell, and so must we. An accurate understanding of this eternal place of torment is a motivating factor to "go and keep on going," telling others the Good News that Jesus saves. He saves us from our own personal destruction, from poverty, from death, and so much more. All of that is good, but most importantly, when we come to Jesus, He saves us from hell. Coming to faith in Christ guarantees us a place in Heaven for all eternity.

We must be fully awake to the fact that people need the Gospel. Your neighbor, your coworkers, and your family members will go to hell if they don't repent and come to faith in Christ. That's simply what the Bible teaches. When you really understand that hell is in front of unsaved people — awaiting them when they die if they fail to accept Christ's sacrifice — you will begin to do everything in your power to keep people from going there.

Ten Things the New Testament Says About Hell

The four gospels in the New Testament tell us many important things about hell. Here are ten specific things we are told about hell — most of which came directly from the lips of Jesus.

1. The Bible tells us hell is *a place of outer darkness*. These are the words Jesus used to describe it in Matthew 25:30.
2. The Bible says hell is *a place of weeping and gnashing of teeth*. Jesus said in Matthew 22:13 that in hell "there shall be weeping and gnashing of teeth." This is a picture of unending mental torture.
3. The Bible says hell is *a place of endless torment*. We read about this in Luke 16:23, where Jesus spoke of the rich man in hell who was in eternal torment — a torment that would never end.
4. The Bible says hell is *a place where men are burned forever with fire and brimstone*. Revelation 21:8 says, "But the fearful, and unbelieving, and the abominable, and murderers, and whoremongers, and sorcerers, and idolaters, and all liars, shall have their part in the lake which burneth with fire and brimstone: which is the second death." Hell is a real place of fire and brimstone. It is not just for murderers, thieves, liars, and sorcerers. It is also for the unbelieving — those who have never come to faith in Christ. They will go to hell.
5. The Bible says hell is *a place where the worm never dies*. Again, Jesus Himself uttered these words in Mark 9:44. This is yet another description of endless torment.
6. The Bible says hell is *a place where the fire is never quenched*. These were also the descriptive words of Jesus found in Mark 9:43 and 44.
7. Similarly in Revelation 9:2, hell is described as *a great furnace*. During the Tribulation, the great furnace will be opened.
8. The Bible says hell is *a place of no rest*. We find this in Revelation 14:11. It says people in hell have no rest day or night.
9. The Bible says hell is *a place of memory*. In Luke 16, Jesus told His disciples the real-life story of the rich man and Lazarus. He said that in

hell, the rich man could remember his past life and past opportunities. In hell, a person will eternally regret and never forget the opportunities he had to repent and accept Christ into his life.

10. The Bible also says hell is *a place a person can never leave.* This too was voiced by Jesus and recorded in Luke 16:26. The rich man wanted Lazarus to bring him a drop of water to cool his tongue, but Jesus said it was impossible. Therefore, hell is a place where people are locked up eternally.

What Do Your Actions Show?

When you really believe that there are only two places people will spend eternity, it will affect your actions. When you get a revelation that hell is a real place where unsaved people all around you are headed, it will give you a sense of urgency to rise up and do something to help rescue the perishing.

James 2:18 says, "A man may say, Thou hast faith, and I have works: shew me thy faith without thy works, and I will shew thee my faith by my works." Our works, or actions, reveal what we really believe.

Do you have a passion for souls? If not, ask the Holy Spirit to give you a revelation of the reality of hell along with a revelation of the saving power of Jesus Christ. Ask Him to empower you to speak the truth in love and always be ready to give a reason to others about the hope you have in Jesus Christ (*see* 1 Peter 3:15).

STUDY QUESTIONS

Study to shew thyself approved unto God, a workman that needeth not to be ashamed, rightly dividing the word of truth.
— 2 Timothy 2:15

1. Many times people will shrink from sharing the Gospel because they're afraid they won't know what to say to someone. Thankfully, God gives us an amazing promise to alleviate this fear, and it is found in three of the gospels: Matthew 10:18-20; Mark 13:11; and Luke 12:11, 12. Carefully read these verses and write out what God is speaking to you personally.

2. After reading through the ten things the New Testament says about hell, what elements had you not heard of prior to this teaching?

Which aspect is most sobering to you? How has this knowledge affected your perspective?

PRACTICAL APPLICATION

> **But be ye doers of the word, and not hearers only, deceiving your own selves.**
> —James 1:22

1. When you have a heart revelation that hell is a real place and people are headed there, you will begin to do whatever you can to tell people about Jesus. Be honest. What do your actions show? Are you sharing your faith with the lost around you when the Holy Spirit gives you opportunity? If not, why not? *Pray and ask the Holy Spirit to give you a passion for souls and opportunities to share the Gospel.*

2. First Peter 3:15 (*TLB*) says, "Quietly trust yourself to Christ your Lord and if anybody asks why you believe as you do, be ready to tell him, and do it in a gentle and respectful way." If you encountered someone who didn't know Jesus, who was about to die, and you thought you might never see him or her again, what would you want to say to that person? God wants you to *be ready* to respectfully give others a reason for your hope in Christ. Take some time to write what you could briefly share with someone in a situation like this.

LESSON 3

TOPIC

A Passion for God's Word

SCRIPTURES

1. **Acts 2:42, 43** — And they continued steadfastly in the apostles' doctrine and fellowship, and in breaking of bread, and in prayers. And fear came upon every soul: and many wonders and signs were done by the apostles.

2. **Matthew 4:23** — And Jesus went about all Galilee, teaching in their synagogues, and preaching the gospel of the kingdom, and healing all manner of sickness and all manner of disease among the people.

3. **Mark 16:20** — And they went forth, and preached every where, the Lord working with them, and confirming the word with signs following.
4. **Acts 8:6, 7** — And the people with one accord gave heed unto those things which Philip spake, hearing and seeing the miracles which he did. For unclean spirits, crying with loud voice, came out of many that were possessed with them: and many taken with palsies, and that were lame, were healed.
5. **1 Peter 1:22, 23** — Seeing ye have purified your souls in obeying the truth.... Being born again, not of corruptible seed, but of incorruptible, by the word of God, which liveth and abideth for ever.
6. **2 Timothy 4:2** — Preach the word; be instant in season, out of season; reprove, rebuke, exhort with all long-suffering and doctrine.
7. **Matthew 24:35** — Heaven and earth shall pass away, but my words shall not pass away.

GREEK WORDS

1. "continued stedfastly" — προσκαρτερέω (*proskartereo*): to persevere consistently; pictures intense focus and hard work; constant diligence and effort that never lets up; can carry the idea of an addiction
2. "preach" — κηρύσσω (*kerusso*): to proclaim, to declare, to announce, or to herald a message; to publish a message; pictures a message proclaimed by the official spokesman or herald of a king, whose job was to announce with a clear and unquestionable voice the desires, dictates, or orders of the king; this was a high, noble, and privileged position
3. "to be instant" — ἐφίστημι (*ephistemi*): to take a firm stand or a hard position; a term borrowed from the military that meant to stay at one's post
4. "in season" — εὔκαιρος (*eukairos*): good times, happy times, pleasing times, enjoyable times, or pleasurable times; something that is timely, suitable, convenient
5. "out of season" — ἀκαίρως (*akairos*): bad times, unhappy times, unpleasing times, unenjoyable times, unpleasurable times; can also mean unfitting or out of place
6. "reprove" — ἐλέγχω (*elegcho*): to convict; to expose, or to cross-examine for the purpose of a conviction, as when convicting a lawbreaker

in a court of law; pictures the image of a lawyer who presents evidence that is indisputable and undeniable so that the accused person's actions are brought to light and, as a result, the offender is exposed and convicted

7. "rebuke" — ἐπιτιμάω (*epitimao*): to chide, to admonish, to warn, or even to correct; describes a frank, but honorable way of politely telling a person that he or she has done something that one perceives to be wrong

8. "exhort" — παρακαλέω (*parakaleo*): to urge, beseech, plead, beg, pray; pictures someone who has come closely alongside another person for the sake of speaking to him, consoling him, comforting him, or assisting him with instruction, counsel, or advice; used to depict military leaders who came alongside their troops to urge, exhort, beseech, beg, and plead with them to stand tall and face their battles bravely

9. "doctrine" — διδαχή (*didache*): the body of Christian teaching

SYNOPSIS

In front of the Moscow Kremlin stands a huge, newly erected statue of Vladimar the Great, who was coronated the prince of Kievan Rus´ in the late Tenth Century. This Grand Prince of Kiev began his reign in a horrible, deeply pagan culture that was steeped in blood sacrifices and other occult activity. But after years of pagan rule, Prince Vladimir became responsible for establishing Christianity among the Russian-speaking people, delivering them from the dark power of those old practices and leading them in an entirely different direction.

This statue of Vladimir commemorates a mass conversion of Russian-speakers to Christianity. Under his rule, a new movement had begun in which the Word of God became venerated. The virtues and values of the Bible began to replace old pagan attitudes. In fact, that love for God's Word affected the culture so greatly that charity replaced treachery on a large scale, and peace subdued chaos and disorder for many, many years.

What about you? Do you love the Bible? Are you inspiring others to love it too? If you're serious about being a successful Christian, you will have to have the Word of God as the anchor of your life. And you'll have to develop *a passion for God's Word*.

The emphasis of this lesson:

The second key ingredient to make you a strong, solid believer is having a passion for the Word of God. It adds consistency to your life in all areas. Where the Bible is active, the supernatural power of the Holy Spirit is active too.

Believers Continued Steadfastly in the Word

The Early Church had a passion for the Word of God, and we read about it throughout the book of Acts. For example, in Acts 2:42 it says, "And they continued steadfastly in the apostles' doctrine and fellowship, and in breaking of bread, and in prayers." The apostles' "doctrine" was the Word of God, and as they were teaching it, the believers "continued steadfastly" in it.

The phrase "continued steadfastly" in the Greek language means *to persevere consistently*. It describes *an intense focus, constant diligence, hard work, and effort that never lets up*. This indicates that believers were consistently in the Word. Their feeding on the Word was not hit or miss, start and stop. It was continual and intense.

Interestingly, the phrase "continued steadfastly" also carries the idea of *an addiction*. It was as if early believers were *addicted* to the apostles' teaching. They gave the Word of God their intense focus, applying every effort to not only hear it, but also to put it into practice. They knew how important it was and how much they needed it.

Jesus was focused intently on the Word in His ministry. In fact, *He was the Word!* Everywhere He went, He taught and expounded on the Scriptures. This was the pattern He established, and the apostles learned it and carried it out in their own ministries. Remember, before they were called apostles, they were called *disciples*. "Disciple" is the Greek word *mathetes*, which carries *the idea of submission to authority*. A better translation of "disciple" would be *a real student or learner*.

That's what the 12 disciples were — they were 12 *learners* who were submitted to the authority of Jesus. They followed Jesus, worked with Jesus, and did the works of Jesus. They observed His absolute commitment to the Word of God, and they developed an absolute commitment to the Word of God too.

Supernatural Signs Accompany God's Word

Matthew 4:23 says, "Jesus went about all Galilee, teaching in their synagogues, and preaching the gospel of the kingdom, and healing all manner of sickness and all manner of disease among the people." What was Jesus teaching and preaching? It was the Word of God. What were the results of the Word going forth? The Scripture says, "…Healing all manner of sickness and all manner of disease among the people."

The Early Church followed Christ's example. They saw that when He taught the Word, the supernatural working of the Holy Spirit was present. Likewise, when they proclaimed the Word, that proclamation was also accompanied by the supernatural signs of the Holy Spirit. We saw in Acts 2:42 that the believers "continued steadfastly in the apostles' doctrine," which was the Word of God. What happened as a result? Verse 43 says, "And fear came upon every soul: and *many wonders and signs were done by the apostles.*" The power of the Holy Spirit manifested Himself commensurate with the proclaiming of the Word.

In Acts 8:6 it says, "The people with one accord gave heed unto those things which Philip spake…." Philip was speaking the Word of God, and when he did, the people began "hearing and seeing the miracles which he did. For unclean spirits, crying with loud voice, came out of many that were possessed with them: and many taken with palsies, and that were lame, were healed" (v. 7).

Again and again, we see this pattern in the Early Church. Where the Word was taught and preached, the Holy Spirit was found working. The same holds true for us today. And the opposite holds true too: If you remove the preaching and teaching of the *Word* of God, you remove the working of the *power* of God — the manifestation of the Holy Spirit.

How the Devil Has Duped Many Churches

In many churches today, the enemy has successfully tricked the leadership into backing away from teaching and preaching the Word of God. Satan knows that where there's no ministry of the Word, there will be very little supernatural work of the Holy Spirit. Regrettably, he has been effective in his efforts.

In place of the Word, many pastors offer inspirational and motivational messages to comfort and encourage the masses. This departure from teaching the Bible has created a large company of churchgoers who are biblically illiterate. If a basic doctrinal test was given in most churches, many members and attendees would fail.

God wants us to dig deeper into His Word, not pull away from it! He wants us to be intelligent, passionate people who esteem and embrace His truth at every opportunity. Believers who are full of the Word are full of Jesus and are empowered to live pure lives.

First Peter 1:22 says, "Seeing ye have *purified* your souls in obeying the truth...." This indicates that without the application of the Word, our souls cannot be purified. What's more, we can't even be born again without the Word. For in the very next verse it says, "Being born again, not of corruptible seed, but of incorruptible, by *the word of God*, which liveth and abideth for ever."

It is no wonder the Early Church was addicted to the Word being taught by the apostles. They understood how vital it was for their spiritual well-being. They knew that if they removed the Word from their lives, they would remove the all-powerful, spiritually transforming action of the Holy Spirit, and they were not willing to do that.

Stay With the Word, and the Word Will Stay With You

In Second Timothy 4:2, Paul instructed Timothy (and the entire Church today) to "preach the word; be instant in season, out of season; reprove, rebuke, exhort with all long suffering and doctrine."

The word "preach" is the Greek word *kerusso*, and it means *to proclaim, to declare, to announce, or to herald a message.* It is the picture of *a message proclaimed by the official spokesman or herald of a king, whose job was to announce with a clear and unquestionable voice the desires, dictates, or orders of the king.* To publish or herald a message was a high, noble, and privileged responsibility. This informs us that there is no greater position or privilege than to be a proclaimer of God's Word. As a herald of the King of kings, our job is to hear what the Word of God says and to declare it distinctly and clearly to others.

How are we to proclaim the Word? Paul says we are to "be instant in season, out of season...." The phrase "be instant" is the Greek word *ephistemi*, which means *to take a firm stand or a hard position*. It is a term borrowed from the military that meant *to stay at one's post*.

At times, believers will be tempted to pull away from their "post" of proclaiming the Word. But God says, "Don't do that! Stay at your post and stay with the Word! Teach it in season and out of season, when times are *favorable* and when times are *not so favorable*."

This phrase "in season" is the Greek word *eukairos*, which means *in good times, happy times, pleasing times, enjoyable times, or pleasurable times*. It indicates *something that is timely, suitable, or convenient*. The phrase "out of season" is the Greek word *akairos*, and it means just the opposite. It indicates *bad times, unhappy times, unpleasing times, unenjoyable times, or unpleasurable times*. It can also mean *something unfitting or out of place*.

Expect Good Results From the Preaching of the Word — Even in 'Reproving' and 'Rebuking'!

Basically, God is saying, "Never veer from the Word. Preach it when things are good, and preach it when things are bad. Don't surrender your position. Declare the Word of God clearly and distinctly so that everyone understands the message. When you do, you can expect good results to follow."

The apostle Paul wrote by the inspiration of the Holy Spirit, "Preach the word; be instant in season, out of season; reprove, rebuke, exhort with all long suffering and doctrine" (2 Timothy 4:2).

Notice the word "reprove." It is the Greek word *elegcho*, meaning *to convict, to expose, or to cross-examine for the purpose of a conviction, as when convicting a lawbreaker in a court of law*. It is *a picture of a lawyer who presents evidence that is indisputable and undeniable so that the accused person's actions are brought to light and, as a result, the offender is exposed and convicted*.

This means when the Word of God is declared, it brings offenders to a place of conviction. It exposes them and what needs to change in their life. It doesn't just pat them on the back and say, "Everything will be fine." On the contrary, the real preaching of the Bible brings forth a sword that "slices open" the human heart. It exposes the condition that people are in so that their condition can be rectified and their lives blessed and improved. This is the first action preaching the Word produces. No wonder the devil hates it!

Next is the word "rebuke." It is the Greek word *epitimao*, and it means *to chide, to admonish, to warn, or even to correct*. This is something many pastors seem reluctant to do. "Rebuke" (*epitimao*) in this verse describes *a frank, but honorable way of politely telling a person that he or she has done something wrong*. Although rebuking does not mean being rude, it does mean speaking the truth with such power and anointing that it brings the offender to a place of total conviction by the Spirit of God.

In addition to *reproving* and *rebuking*, the Word of God will also "exhort" us. The word "exhort" is the Greek word *parakaleo*, which means *to urge, beseech, plead, beg, or pray*. It is the motivational aspect of preaching. It is *the picture of someone who has come closely alongside another for the sake of consoling him, comforting him, or assisting him with instruction, counsel, or advice*. This word "exhort" was used to depict *military leaders who came alongside their troops to urge, exhort, beseech, beg, and plead with them to stand tall and face their battles bravely*.

All these results can be expected from the preaching and teaching of the Word of God. The Word *reproves, rebukes,* and *exhorts* and it does so with longsuffering and doctrine. The word "doctrine" is the Greek word *didache*, and it describes the whole body of Christian teaching. When we teach, we are to teach the whole Bible, not just the selective parts we like.

When all these things are done effectively — either by the pastor in the pulpit or by you as you share the Word with others — the Holy Spirit will pull out His divine scalpel and slice into the human heart to correct us and remove from our lives what needs to be removed. Using the Word, He does His surgical work on our hearts and souls like nothing and no one else can.

As the Word goes forth, each listener receives exactly what he or she needs in that moment. One receives reproof, another rebuke, another faith, and another exhortation. In one moment, the Holy Spirit miraculously and simultaneously tailors the message and performs a unique work in the heart of every hearer. This is an absolute supernatural work of the Holy Spirit that takes place when the Word is powerfully and clearly declared. No wonder the devil hates the teaching of the Bible. He doesn't want these works of God to happen in you, in your friends, or in your church.

A Warning for the Last Days

The Holy Spirit explicitly warns us in Second Timothy 4:3 and 4 that in the latter times people will grow weary of the Word of God and will begin to depart from it. Knowing that this is a trend the enemy is baiting people — even believers — to buy into, we have to be careful that we don't become a victim to the spirit of the age.

Just because others are discarding the Bible doesn't mean you should. Instead, tighten the belt of truth around your life (*see* Ephesians 6:14). Like the Early Church, become addicted to the Word, and the supernatural working of the Holy Spirit will be present in *your* life.

Jesus said, "Heaven and earth shall pass away, but my words shall not pass away" (Matthew 24:35). Nothing will outlast the Word of God — nothing. God's Word is eternal, impervious, unchangeable, immutable, and *forever settled*! Rather than shy away from it or discard it, you need to embrace it. It is an essential ingredient that will empower you to be strong, mature, and stable throughout your life.

STUDY QUESTIONS

Study to shew thyself approved unto God, a workman that needeth not to be ashamed, rightly dividing the word of truth.
— 2 Timothy 2:15

1. Jesus said, "…If ye continue in my word, then are ye my disciples indeed; and ye shall know the truth, and the truth shall make you free" (John 8:31, 32). Stop and think about a verse or passage of Scripture that has brought great freedom to your life? Write it out and share how the Holy Spirit has used it to bring more light, liberty, and life to you and your situation.

2. One of the most amazing things about the Word of God is its inherent power. Hebrews 4:12 communicates this clearly. Take a moment and meditate on this verse in a few different Bible versions. Write out the version that impacts you most. What is the Holy Spirit speaking to you in this scripture?

PRACTICAL APPLICATION

> **But be ye doers of the word, and not hearers only, deceiving your own selves.**
> **—James 1:22**

1. Throughout the early New Testament, supernatural signs accompanied the teaching, preaching, and sharing of God's Word. Healings, miracles, and wonders of all kinds were manifested and witnessed. Imagine for a moment what life would be like if these kinds of signs were present every time *you* declared God's Word. How do you think it would affect unbelievers? How would it affect you personally?
2. Believers in the Early Church "continued steadfastly" in the Word of God. That is, they had *an intense focus, constant diligence, and a sustained effort to learn and apply it in their lives.* They were *addicted* to it. Have you ever experienced this level of passion for the Word? If so, what form sparked your excitement (written Word, audio Bible, sermon, etc.)? How can you create more space for hearing, receiving, and applying God's Word in your life?

LESSON 4

TOPIC

A Passion for the Holy Spirit — Part 1

SCRIPTURES

1. **1 Corinthians 14:1** — Follow after charity, and desire spiritual gifts....

GREEK WORDS

1. "desire" — ζηλόω (*zeloo*): a word intended to imitate the sound of boiling water; to bubble over because something is so hot; to burn with zeal; to be earnest; to set one's heart on; to be completely intent upon; it is where we get the word "zeal"

SYNOPSIS

Something extraordinary happened right on the very edge of Red Square in Moscow, Russia. It was not something that happened thousands or even hundreds of years ago. It was something that happened just in the year 2000. At that time, the Hotel Russia, located on the edge of Red Square, became our Moscow Good News Church home, and we began meeting there every week. During every service, the place was packed with people who were genuinely hungry for the Word of God. Many were saved and filled with the Holy Spirit, and we saw the power of the Holy Spirit demonstrated again and again. Our church was birthed in the power of the Holy Spirit.

If there's anything that is needed in the earth today, it is the work of the Holy Spirit! In this lesson, we'll begin looking at the power of the Person and work of the Holy Spirit that is so necessary in *every* believer's life.

The emphasis of this lesson:

In order to be a truly successful believer, you need a passion for the Person and the work of the Holy Spirit. God wants you to desire the operation of His gifts in your life, your church, and your community in the same way He operated in the Early Church.

So far, we've learned two of the ten ingredients required to be strong and victorious in this life: 1) *a passion for souls*; and 2) *a passion for the Word of God*. We know that where the Word is taught and preached, the supernatural working of the Holy Spirit is found. This truth takes us into today's lesson — having a *passion for the work of the Holy Spirit*.

Jesus and the Holy Spirit Are Inseparable

The believers in the First Century had a passion for the Holy Spirit's power and for experiencing His gifts at work among them. We see this throughout the book of Acts. Yet no one on earth knew the Holy Spirit better and more intimately than Jesus Himself.

How connected were Jesus and the Holy Spirit? *They were completely connected.* From the beginning of His life in His earthly ministry through the end of His life and His resurrection, Christ was inseparably connected with the Person and power of the Holy Spirit.

Just look at this quick list of the intimate role the Spirit played in Jesus' life.

- Jesus was *conceived* by the Holy Spirit in the womb of the virgin Mary (*see* Matthew 1:20).
- Jesus was *baptized* by the Holy Spirit at the Jordan River (*see* Matthew 3:16).
- Jesus was *led* by the Holy Spirit before, during, and after His testing in the wilderness (*see* Luke 4:14).
- Jesus was *empowered* to minister by the Holy Spirit (*see* Luke 4:18, 19).
- Jesus *cast out demons* by the power of the Holy Spirit (*see* Matthew 12:28).
- Jesus *healed* others by the power of the Holy Spirit (*see* Luke 5:17).
- Jesus *taught* about the Holy Spirit (*see* John chapters 14-16).
- Jesus *offered Himself up* and was *crucified* in the power of the Holy Spirit (*see* Hebrews 9:14).
- Jesus was *raised from the dead* by the power of the Holy Spirit (*see* Romans 8:11).

Before His final ascension into Heaven, Jesus *promised* the Baptism in the Holy Spirit to His disciples (*see* Acts 1:8). These were His last words. Once at the Father's right hand, He *poured out the gift* of the Holy Spirit (*see* Acts 2:33). This was His first act after He took His place next to the Father. From the beginning to the end of His life in His earthly ministry, Jesus and the Holy Spirit were inseparable. Everything Christ did, He did in partnership with the Spirit.

Should we expect to be successful if we do anything less?

The Disciples Mirrored Their Master

We learned that the first 12 individuals Jesus chose to accompany Him in the ministry were first called "disciples." The word "disciple" is the Greek word *mathetes*, which essentially means *learners*. It carries the idea of *a student who is completely submitted to his master and will do anything that is requested*. The disciple's job was to duplicate whatever the master did. All of this meaning is inherent in the word "disciple."

The disciples watched Jesus, walked with Jesus, and ministered with Jesus for more than three years. They saw His total dependence on the Holy

Spirit, and everything He did, they replicated in their own lives and ministries.

Once Jesus ascended into Heaven, these 12 disciples became the original apostles, and their apostolic ministries began in full force. They did what Jesus did:

- They ministered in the power of the Holy Spirit.
- They preached the Word in the power of the Holy Spirit.
- They healed the sick in the power of the Holy Spirit.

Everything the apostles did, they did in partnership with the Holy Spirit — just as their Master Jesus Christ had clearly demonstrated.

The apostles had an addiction to the Holy Spirit's ministry! They understood that if they tried to do anything without Him, their efforts would be futile and fruitless.

Interestingly, the Holy Spirit is mentioned 56 times in the four gospels and 57 times in the book of Acts alone. The Spirit is mentioned 112 times in Paul's epistles and another 36 times in the remaining books of the New Testament. When you add it all up, you will discover 261 references to the Holy Spirit in the New Testament. This signifies the major importance of the doctrine of the Holy Spirit. Since the Holy Spirit is referred to so frequently, how vital do you think He should be in *your* life?

Ten Symbolic Depictions of the Spirit

From Genesis to Revelation, the Holy Spirit is symbolically depicted in ten different forms.

1. The Holy Spirit is depicted as *oil*. He is oil because He anoints us (*see* Psalm 92:10).
2. The Holy Spirit is described as *dew* (*see* Psalm 133:1-3). The Bible says the anointing is like the dew of Mount Hermon. Dew appears in the morning, and when it appears it covers everything. Likewise, when the Holy Spirit is described as dew, it signifies the corporate anointing that is on an entire unified congregation or group. This "dew" of the Holy Spirit is a manifestation of the Spirit suddenly showing up — everywhere, on everything.

3. The Holy Spirit is referred to as *water* (*see* Isaiah 44:3). The Bible says God will pour His Spirit out like water upon hearts that are hungry and thirsty for more of Him.
4. The Holy Spirit is also referred to as *fire* (*see* Luke 3:16). He often burns up the things in our lives that are *not* like Jesus, but sets powerfully ablaze the things that *are* like Him.
5. The Holy Spirit is described as *a dove* (*see* Matthew 3:16). The Bible never says the Holy Spirit *is* a dove. It says the Holy Spirit descended upon Jesus *like* a dove. A dove is gentle and peaceful. The dove depicts the gentleness of the Holy Spirit.
6. The Holy Spirit is also referred to as *a river* (*see* John 7:37-39). A river is moving, flowing, and bubbling up to give life. The Holy Spirit is like a river to those who will allow Him to flow in their lives.
7. The Holy Spirit is called *wind* (*see* John 3:8). Jesus compared Him with wind in His conversation with Nicodemus, and we see the Holy Spirit appearing as wind in the upper room (*see* Acts 2:2). Wind is very powerful and can be very noisy.
8. The Holy Spirit is called *a seal* (*see* 2 Corinthians 1:22). In our salvation, the Holy Spirit seals us up in Christ.
9. The Holy Spirit is also called *an earnest* (*see* 2 Corinthians 1:22). This is another word for *down payment*. The Holy Spirit is God's *down payment* guaranteeing that Heaven is in our future.
10. Lastly, the Holy Spirit is called *wine*. In Ephesians 5:18, the Bible says, "Be not drunk with wine, wherein is excess; but be filled with the Spirit." The Holy Spirit can have a positive "inebriating" effect on our lives.

When you're filled with the Holy Spirit, He changes the way you feel and the perspective in which you see things. Everything changes when you are filled with the Holy Spirit. That's because He is God's wine for the believer.

How can you anticipate the Holy Spirit showing up and moving in your life, in your family, or in your church? That list provided at least ten possibilities. Yet exactly what He does is unique to each person. We see a glimpse of this throughout the book of Acts.

The Book of Acts: A Pattern for the Church

The book of Acts was written by Luke, and this book not only contains the history of the Early Church, but it is also *a pattern* for the Church of all generations. What happened in Acts is what is supposed to be happening in the life of every believer and every church throughout all generations.

For example, in Acts 1:8, Jesus' last words before His ascension were a promise that the Holy Spirit's power would be available to all believers. He said, "But ye shall receive power, after that the Holy Ghost is come upon you...."

In Acts 2:4, His words were fulfilled. It says, "And they were all filled with the Holy Ghost, and began to speak with other tongues, as the Spirit gave them utterance." Never underestimate the power of speaking in other tongues. When you speak in other tongues, it moves you into a supernatural dimension.

In Acts 2:42 and 43, which we examined in our last lesson, we see the pattern of the Holy Spirit working whenever the Word of God is preached, taught, or proclaimed. In Acts 3:6-8, we see the Holy Spirit working through Peter and John as they laid their hands on the lame man near the temple, and the man was instantly healed. Then in Acts 4:31, we find the Holy Spirit showing up at a prayer meeting, baptizing all who were in attendance with a boldness to speak God's Word.

In Acts 5:12-15, we see the Holy Spirit working through the apostles so powerfully that not only were they laying hands on people and the people were getting well, but even the sick who were laid in the path of *Peter's shadow* received healing.

Signs and wonders of the Spirit continued in Acts 6:8 at the hands of Stephen. The apostle Philip was also used mightily by the Holy Spirit among the people in the city of Samaria. Scripture says, "For unclean spirits, crying with loud voice, came out of many that were possessed with them: and many taken with palsies, and that were lame, were healed" (Acts 8:7).

When we come to Acts 10:44-46, we see the Holy Spirit move in an unprecedented way. For the first time ever, Gentiles were baptized in the

Holy Spirit and began to speak with other tongues. The centurion Cornelius and his entire household were saved and filled with the Holy Spirit.

The gift of prophecy was in operation through a believer named Agabus in Acts 11:28, and in Acts 13:2 the Holy Spirit directed the church leaders at Antioch to separate Barnabas and Saul (Paul) for the special ministry to which He had called them.

Looking at Acts 14:8-10, we see the Holy Spirit's gift of healing working through Paul. As Paul preached in Lystra, a man crippled from birth had faith to be healed. When Paul saw him, he said, "Stand upright on thy feet. And he leaped and walked" (v. 10).

In Acts 16:7 and 8, Paul's ministry team experienced the working of the Spirit's gift of prophecy. When they came to Mysia and were preparing to go into Bithynia, the Holy Spirit would not give them peace about proceeding.

By the time we get to Acts 19, approximately 24 years had passed since the Day of Pentecost. Paul was making a return visit to the city of Ephesus, and he encountered a group of John the Baptist's disciples. After leading them to salvation in Christ, he laid hands on them to receive the baptism in the Holy Spirit. Immediately, they were all filled with the Spirit and began speaking in other tongues *and* prophesying (v. 6). Again, this was 24 years after Pentecost. More than two decades later, believers were still laying hands on people, and they were still being baptized in the Holy Spirit!

Again and again, we see the same kinds of things happening throughout Acts. The Lord gave us this book as a pattern of what is supposed to happen in the life of every believer and every church throughout all generations.

Desire Spiritual Gifts

Some have taught that it is wrong to seek supernatural manifestations, but that is not true. Not only is it right to seek them, God encourages us to do so. In First Corinthians 14:1, we are told to "Follow after charity, and desire spiritual gifts...." The word "charity" is the Greek word *agape*. A better translation of the opening of this verse would be "follow after love." Most would agree that following after love is a good thing, and it is.

But that is not all this verse instructs us to do. In addition to following after love, we are to "desire spiritual gifts...." The word "desire" is the Greek word *zeloo*, and it is *a word intended to imitate the sound of boiling water*. It means *to bubble over because something is so hot; to burn with zeal; to be deeply committed to a thing; to set one's heart on something*. It is where we get the word "zeal."

When the apostle Paul tells us to "desire spiritual gifts," it literally means we're to be bubbling over with zeal for the gifts of the Holy Spirit. We are to be deeply committed to the operation of spiritual gifts and to be earnest about them. We're to set our heart upon them and be completely zealous when it comes to operating in this supernatural dimension — in the work of the Holy Spirit.

If there is no miraculous working of the Holy Spirit in your life, you will probably experience frustration, marginal fruit, and very little power. That is why it is essential for you to have a passion for the Holy Spirit in your life. He will help you be a strong, mature believer, ready for whatever comes your way.

STUDY QUESTIONS

> **Study to shew thyself approved unto God, a workman that needeth not to be ashamed, rightly dividing the word of truth.**
> **— 2 Timothy 2:15**

1. The Holy Spirit played an intimate role in the life of Jesus. Carefully read through the list that details how they were inseparably connected. What aspects were you surprised to see in that list? Why? Overall, what does this speak to you personally about the need for the Holy Spirit's involvement in *your* life? (Also consider Zechariah 4:6; John 6:63; 15:5; Romans 7:18; and 2 Corinthians 3:5.)
2. If you have not experienced the baptism in the Holy Spirit but would like to, the promises of Acts 2:38 and 39 and Luke 11:9-13 will be encouraging for you to read. What is the Holy Spirit speaking to you in these passages?

PRACTICAL APPLICATION

> **But be ye doers of the word, and not hearers only, deceiving your own selves.**
> **— James 1:22**

1. Be honest. How much do you *rely on* and *include* the Holy Spirit's help and friendship in your daily life? What do you regularly ask Him for help with? How has He specifically helped you do what you could never have done on your own?
2. What area(s) of your life have you *not* asked Him for help with in the past, but you plan on inviting Him to help you with moving forward?
3. First Corinthians 14:1 instructs us to "desire spiritual gifts." This literally means we're to be bubbling over with zeal for the gifts of the Holy Spirit. We're to be deeply committed to the operation of spiritual gifts and to be *earnes*t about them. After hearing this definition of the word "desire," would you say that *you* desire spiritual gifts? If not, why not? How has this lesson changed your perspective on this subject?

LESSON 5

TOPIC
A Passion for the Holy Spirit — Part 2

SCRIPTURES

1. **1 Corinthians 1:4-9** — I thank my God always on your behalf, for the grace of God which is given you by Jesus Christ; that in every thing ye are enriched by him, in all utterance, and in all knowledge; even as the testimony of Christ was confirmed in you: so that ye come behind in no gift; waiting for the coming of our Lord Jesus Christ: who shall also confirm you unto the end, that ye may be blameless in the day of our Lord Jesus Christ. God is faithful, by whom ye were called unto the fellowship of his Son Jesus Christ our Lord.
2. **1 Corinthians 14:1** — Follow after charity, and desire spiritual gifts….
3. **1 Timothy 4:14** — Neglect not the gift that is in thee, which was given thee by prophecy, with the laying on of the hands of the presbytery.
4. **2 Timothy 1:6** — Wherefore I put thee in remembrance that thou stir up the gift of God, which is in thee by the putting on of my hands.

5. **1 Corinthians 12:7** — But the manifestation of the Spirit is given to every man to profit withal.
6. **1 Corinthians 14:26** — How is it then, brethren? When ye come together, every one of you hath a psalm, hath a doctrine, hath a tongue, hath a revelation, hath an interpretation. Let all things be done unto edifying.

GREEK WORDS

1. "desire" — ζηλόω (*zeloo*): a word intended to imitate the sound of boiling water; to bubble over because something is so hot; to burn with zeal; to be earnest; to set one's heart on; to be completely intent upon; it is where we get the word zeal
2. "neglect" — ἀμελέω (*ameleo*): to treat as unimportant; to treat as having no value; to view as insignificant
3. "stir up" — ἀναζωπυρέω (*anadzopureo*): to rekindle; to inflame; to stir up as bellows are used to rekindle a fire
4. "every man" — ἕκαστος (*hekastos*): an all-inclusive term that embraces everyone, with no one excluded
5. "edifying" — οἰκοδομή (*oikodome*): an architectural term meaning to enlarge or amplify a house; depicts following an architectural plan to enlarge, increase, or amplify; to improve; to leave in an improved condition

SYNOPSIS

The Moscow Good News Church is a beautiful place to worship God and experience His presence each week. People flood the auditorium every time the doors are opened. They have a passion for the Word of God and a passion for the moving of the Holy Spirit. When Russian people get saved, they love the supernatural working of the Holy Spirit. It is a joy to witness!

There is one major challenge among this thriving congregation, and that is giving the Holy Spirit enough time to move and minister to the people. This is the case in many churches today. But in addition to creating multiple services to make room for the people, we also need to make room for the Holy Spirit to move and minister to them. This is not optional, but *mandatory*. He is the most important Person in the Church. By making room for the Holy Spirit to move, we make room for the people to receive exactly what they need.

The emphasis of this lesson:

In addition to having a passion for souls and a passion for the Word of God, you need a passion for the Holy Spirit, including a deep desire to see the manifestation of His gifts and His supernatural work. To experience the Spirit's moving, we must make room for Him.

The believers in the Early Church had a genuine passion for the work of the Holy Spirit, and we see Him mightily moving in and through their lives. This is clearly visible throughout the book of Acts. Not only does Acts provide a detailed history of the Church, it also provides a pattern for every church and every believer throughout all generations. The occurrences recorded in the pages of Acts should be happening in the lives of believers today.

The Church of Corinth Flowed Mightily in the Gifts

No New Testament church knew more about the gifts of the Holy Spirit than the church of Corinth. This is clearly confirmed in First Corinthians 1:4-9. In verse 4, the apostle Paul said, "I thank my God always on your behalf, for the grace of God which is given you by Jesus Christ."

The word "grace" here is the Greek word *charis*, and it describes here *God's supernatural touch that empowers us to be different*. It is the touch of the Holy Spirit Himself in our lives. The Corinthians were experiencing this regularly and in abundance!

In verse 5 Paul said, "That in every thing ye are enriched by him, in all utterance, and in all knowledge." The word "enriched" is the Greek word *plousios*, and it describes someone with so much *wealth*, he is not sure exactly how much he has! Paul used this word to describe how many manifestations of the Holy Spirit the Corinthian church was experiencing.

When it came to the operations of the Holy Spirit, the believers in Corinth were overwhelmingly rich. There were just too many occurrences to track, and Paul commended them for this. They were enriched "in all utterance, and in all knowledge." The *utterance* gifts of the Spirit include *speaking in tongues*, *interpretation of tongues*, and *prophecy*. The *knowledge* gifts include the *word of wisdom*, *word of knowledge*, and *discerning of spirits*.

The Gifts of the Spirit Make Jesus More Real to People

In verse 6, Paul continued, "Even as the testimony of Christ was confirmed in you." The "testimony of Christ" is what Jesus did during His life on earth. He was Healer, Prophet, and Miracle-Worker. These things and more are recorded in Scripture, and we believe them about Jesus, as did the Corinthians. But when the gifts of the Holy Spirit are in operation, the Spirit takes what we know about Jesus in the realm of our mind — because of what we read in Scripture — and brings it out into the realm of our present reality.

The Corinthians believed what they had heard about Jesus, but the working of the Holy Spirit in their midst brought the Person of Jesus alive before their very eyes. The same is true for you. When the gift of healing is in operation, the Holy Spirit takes the image of Jesus as Healer out of the "invisible" realm of history and brings it into your present-day reality. The Holy Spirit desires to do this with every aspect of Jesus' character.

The gifts of the Holy Spirit "confirm" the testimony of Christ. The word "confirm" in the Greek means *to authenticate, establish, or make real*. The gifts of the Holy Spirit *make Jesus real* to us! This is why having a passion for the Holy Spirit is so important.

'Second to None' — God's Intent for All People for All Generations

In First Corinthians 1:7, Paul said, "So that ye come behind in no gift; waiting for the coming of our Lord Jesus Christ." The phrase "come behind" in Greek means *to have no deficit of spiritual gifts*. In other words, the believers at Corinth were *second to none* when it came to the gifts of the Holy Spirit.

Verse 7 also tells us how long God intended the gifts of the Spirit to be in operation. Paul said, "…Waiting for the coming of our Lord Jesus Christ." In other words, the gifts were not just meant for the Early Church in the First Century. Rather, the gifts are for *all* of God's people for *all* generations. They are meant to be in operation until "the coming of the Lord Jesus."

The Body of Christ today needs the supernatural presence and working of the Holy Spirit just as much as the Early Church did. One of the reasons is that the workings of the Holy Spirit "…shall also confirm you unto the end, that ye may be blameless in the day of our Lord Jesus Christ" (v. 8). The word "end" is the Greek word *telos*, and it describes *something that is ripe or mature*. When the gifts of the Spirit are in operation, they bring us into new levels of spiritual maturity. Without the gifts of the Spirit, we cannot grow properly.

The Gifts of the Spirit Bring Us Into Partnership With Jesus

In First Corinthians 1:9, the apostle Paul said, "God is faithful, by whom ye were called unto the fellowship of his Son Jesus Christ our Lord." The word "fellowship" is the Greek word *koinonia*. It describes *real, legitimate business partners who work together in business*. It is the same word used in Luke 5:7 when Peter called his fishing "partners" to help him haul in the miraculous catch.

What Paul is saying here is that when the gifts of the Holy Spirit are in operation, they bring us into *real, legitimate partnership with Jesus Christ Himself*! Could anything be more valuable, more exciting, or more life-changing than being in this kind of "fellowship" (*koinonia*) with Jesus?

The subject of spiritual gifts was so vital that the apostle Paul devoted three entire chapters in First Corinthians to the subject: chapters 12, 13, and 14. These chapters include more than 100 verses on the Holy Spirit and His supernatural gifts working in the Church! He added to these verses further instruction in Romans 12. This tells us that if we want to be the power-filled Christians God wants us to be, we need to have a passion for the working of the Holy Spirit.

Be Informed About Spiritual Gifts

In First Corinthians 12:1, Paul said, "Now concerning spiritual gifts, brethren, I would not have you ignorant." The word "ignorant" is the Greek word *agnosis*, which means *uninformed*. A literal translation of this could read, "I don't want you to be stupid or ignorant when it comes to the subject of spiritual gifts."

Paul was so adamant about the importance of spiritual gifts that he said in First Corinthians 14:1, "Follow after charity, and *desire* spiritual gifts...." In our last lesson, we learned that the word "desire" is the Greek word *zeloo*, which is a word intended to imitate the sound of boiling water. It means *to bubble over, to be hot for something, to burn with zeal, to be deeply committed to a thing, to be earnest, to set one's heart on something, or to be completely intent on having something*. It is where we get the word "zeal." Therefore, we are to follow after love and boil over with zeal for spiritual gifts. This is not wrong or fanatical or selfish! In fact, to have such desire is *encouraged* by God and *blessed* by God.

In First Timothy 4:14, Paul expressed a similar sense of urgency concerning the gifts of the Spirit. He told young Timothy — and us, "Neglect not the gift that is in thee, which was given thee by prophecy, with the laying on of the hands of the presbytery." We are not to "neglect" the gifts of the Spirit. The word "neglect" is the Greek word *ameleo*, which basically means *to treat as unimportant, invaluable, or insignificant*. In other words, Paul was saying, "Do not treat as unimportant the gifts of the Holy Spirit!"

To make sure we get the point, Paul gives a very similar directive in Second Timothy 1:6. He declared, "Wherefore I put thee in remembrance that thou stir up the gift of God, which is in thee by the putting on of my hands." The phrase "stir up" is the Greek word *anadzopureo*, and it means *to rekindle, to inflame, or to stir up as bellows are used to rekindle a fire*. In other words, God wants you to stoke the coals of the spiritual gifts inside of you. Don't let them go out; instead, fan them into flames.

The Gifts of the Holy Spirit Are for Everyone

Who are the gifts of the Spirit for? *Everyone*. First Corinthians 12:7 says, "But the manifestation of the Spirit is given to *every man* to profit withal." The phrase "every man" is the Greek word *hekastos*, which *is an all-inclusive term that embraces everyone, with no one excluded*. God wants you and *every* believer to flow in the gifts of the Holy Spirit.

This truth is reiterated in First Corinthians 14:26 where the apostle Paul said, "How is it then, brethren? When ye come together, *every one* of you hath a psalm, hath a doctrine, hath a tongue, hath a revelation, hath an interpretation. Let all things be done unto edifying." The phrase "every one" is again the Greek word *hekastos*, meaning *no one is excluded*.

It is also important to note that Paul didn't correct the Corinthians and tell them not to operate in the gifts. On the contrary, he said, "…Let all things be done *unto edifying*" (1 Corinthians 14:26). The condition in which the gifts were to operate was "unto edifying." This phrase is translated from the Greek word *oikodome*, and it is an architectural term meaning *to enlarge or amplify a house*. It depicts someone following an architectural plan *to enlarge, increase, amplify, or to leave in an improved condition*.

When you operate in the gifts of the Holy Spirit, you will be spiritually enlarged. Your capacity for the things of God and His presence will increase. Moreover, when the gifts of the Spirit are working among us, they improve us, leaving our condition better as a result of their operation.

Clearly, we need to regularly make room for the Holy Spirit to work in and through our lives, personally and collectively. As we desire spiritual gifts and do not neglect them, we will become strong, mature believers moving powerfully in the things of God.

STUDY QUESTIONS

> **Study to shew thyself approved unto God, a workman that needeth not to be ashamed, rightly dividing the word of truth.**
> **— 2 Timothy 2:15**

1. The Bible reveals nine specific *gifts* of the Holy Spirit as well as nine specific *fruits*. Read First Corinthians 12:8-10 and Galatians 5:22, 23 to identify these. What do you think the difference is between the *gifts* and the *fruit* of the Spirit?
2. According to First Corinthians 12:7 and First Peter 4:10, God has given us the gifts of His Spirit to strengthen us and bring maturity to the Church. Carefully read First Corinthians 12:12-26. What is the Holy Spirit showing you to always keep in mind when it comes to operating in the gifts?

PRACTICAL APPLICATION

> **But be ye doers of the word, and not hearers only, deceiving your own selves.**
> **— James 1:22**

1. You have probably read or heard about Jesus as the Healer, Miracle-Worker, Truth-Revealer, Provider, and more. But what aspects of His character have you *personally* experienced? That is, in what specific ways has the Holy Spirit made the Person of Jesus come alive before your very eyes?
2. Many have been taught that the gifts of the Holy Spirit are "immature," but that is incorrect. Think back to when you first came to Christ. What were you initially taught about the Holy Spirit and His gifts? How is this lesson opening your spiritual eyes to a deeper, more accurate understanding of the Spirit?
3. In order to experience the work of the Holy Spirit in your life, you need to *make room for Him*. Pause and pray: "Holy Spirit, in what specific ways have I not made room for You to work in my life? Have I neglected Your gifts within me, or have I kept them stirred up? Moving forward, what can I do to make room for You to move in my life and in my church in greater ways?" Be still and listen. What is the Holy Spirit speaking to you?

LESSON 6

TOPIC

A Passion for Worship — Part 1

SCRIPTURES

1. **Acts 2:46, 47** — And they, continuing daily with one accord in the temple, and breaking bread from house to house, did eat their meat with gladness and singleness of heart, praising God, and having favor with with all the people. And the Lord added to the church daily such as should be saved.
2. **Matthew 26:30; Mark 14:26** — And when they had sung an hymn, they went out into the mount of Olives.

3. **Psalm 22:3** — But thou art holy, O thou that inhabitest the praises of Israel.
4. **Psalm 133:1-3** — Behold, how good and how pleasant it is for brethren to dwell together in unity! It is like the precious ointment upon the head, that ran down upon the beard, even Aaron's beard: that went down to the skirts of his garments; as the dew of Hermon, and as the dew that descended upon the mountains of Zion: for there the LORD commanded the blessing, even life for evermore.
5. **Ephesians 5:14** — Wherefore he saith, Awake thou that sleepest, and arise from the dead, and Christ shall give thee light.
6. **Colossians 1:15-20** — Who is the image of the invisible God, the firstborn of every creature: For by him were all things created, that are in heaven, and that are in earth, visible and invisible, whether they be thrones, or dominions, or principalities, or powers: all things were created by him, and for him: And he is before all things, and by him all things consist. And he is the head of the body, the church: who is the beginning, the firstborn from the dead; that in all things he might have the preeminence. For it pleased the Father that in him should all fullness dwell;
7. **Philippians 2:9, 10** — Wherefore God also hath highly exalted him, and given him a name which is above every name: That at the name of Jesus every knee should bow, of things in heaven, and things in earth, and things under the earth.
8. **2 Timothy 2:11-13** — It is a faithful saying: For if we be dead with him, we shall also live with him: If we suffer, we shall also reign with him: if we deny him, he also will deny us: If we believe not, yet he abideth faithful: he cannot deny himself.
9. **Acts 16:25 (*NKJV*)** — But at midnight Paul and Silas were praying and singing hymns to God, and the prisoners were listening to them.

GREEK WORDS

1. "worship" — προσκυνέω (*proskuneo*): to worship; to adore; to fall forward upon one's knees and to kiss; it is a depiction of intimate adoration

SYNOPSIS

Located in the heart of Moscow, Russia, is the Tchaikovsky Music Conservatory. You may be familiar with Tchaikovsky's music. He wrote many notable works including *Swan Lake*, *The Sleeping Beauty*, and *The Nutcracker*. Indeed, Tchaikovsky is a celebrated composer and musician, and the Tchaikovsky Music Conservatory is a well-deserved foundation named in his honor.

Many famous musicians have studied and graduated from this institution, including members of the Moscow Good News Church. These professionals are highly skilled and excellent musicians who are utilizing what they have learned in the worship of God.

Worship has been a very important factor in the life of God's people throughout the Bible. David was a serious worshiper who taught the people of Israel with his psalms how to worship the Lord. His influence can be seen in the life of Christ, Paul, and in New Testament believers. Where there is sincere worship, there you will find the very presence of God inhabiting the praise of His people (*see* Psalm 22:3).

The emphasis of this lesson:

Having a passion for worship is another vital ingredient to being a strong, stable, mature believer. Worship is the intimate adoration of God. When you worship Him, He will literally inhabit your praises, bringing His glory to meet your every need.

The Practice of Worship Was Passed From One Generation to the Next

In the Old Testament, we read that David and Solomon put forth their best efforts into praising and worshiping God. From the praise and worship that accompanied the Ark of the Covenant's return to Jerusalem to the dedication of Solomon's temple, these two leaders developed a whole system of expressing gratitude and adoration to God. Their efforts became a model for the Jewish people to follow. In fact, it became engrained in their hearts. What they developed was eventually passed on to the early New Testament Church and beyond.

Jesus Himself was a worshiper. What He learned and put into practice had been passed down from the generations that preceded Him. In Mark 14:26

and Matthew 26:30, Jesus had just finished serving His disciples the "Last Supper" (what would later become known as the Communion elements) and washing their feet in the upper room. Jesus was just hours away from being crucified, and the Bible says, "And when they had sung an hymn, they went out into the mount of Olives."

Jesus taught His disciples by example how to worship. Remember, the word "disciple" is the Greek word *mathetes*, which describes *a student who is completely submitted to the authority of his master*. The student's job is to replicate everything he sees his master do. In this case, the disciples replicated the way in which Jesus worshiped.

When the Church began in Acts 2, the followers of Christ continued to replicate His established pattern. Not only did they preach like Jesus, heal people like Jesus, cast out demons like Jesus, and flow in the power of the Spirit like Jesus, they also worshiped like Jesus. They were a singing, praising, worshiping Church from their inception. Acts 2:46 and 47 says, "And they, continuing daily with one accord in the temple, and breaking bread from house to house, did eat their meat with gladness and singleness of heart, *praising God*, and having favor with with all the people. And the Lord added to the church daily such as should be saved."

What It Means To Worship

The word "worship" in the New Testament is the Greek word *proskuneo*, which means *to worship, to adore, to fall forward on one's knees and to kiss*. It is a depiction of *intimate adoration*. It literally means to *fall on the knees as an expression of reverence; to prostrate yourself — physically or mentally — in front of God to worship or to make supplication*.

This word "worship" — *proskuneo* — is a very intimate word. It describes entering into a time of deep intimacy with God. Think about your times of worship. Are they intimate moments when you in your heart are falling before God and blowing Him kisses? Worship should be a time of intimacy with the Father that is special and cherished.

God Inhabits Your Praise

In Psalm 22:3, God gives us an amazing promise. The verse says, "But thou art holy, O thou that *inhabitest* the praises of Israel." The word "inhabitest" means *to sit enthroned*. It literally describes the *presence of God sitting on top of a congregation* or *the presence of God literally sitting on top of a believer who is praising and worshiping Him.*

One translation of this verse says, "You sit enthroned on the praises of Israel." When a church or a person enters into a time of worship, that worship creates an atmosphere so wonderful and welcoming to God that He shows up. His supernatural presence is magnetically drawn to the worship, and He literally sits on top of the praise and the worship of that congregation or individual. And when He does, He brings His glory with Him.

Experiencing God's Glory

When the glory of God comes into a congregation or an individual believer's life, it is amazing. Why? With God's glory comes *everything good* that one could ever need in life.

In the Old Testament, the word "glory" is a Hebrew word that denotes the idea of *heaviness and weight*. It actually describes the heavy and weighty presence of God — a presence that is loaded with everything good that we need to change and transform us. In the presence of God's glory are miracles, healings, deliverance, personal inward changes, and everything else we need. His glory is heavy and weighty with goodness. That's the meaning of the word "glory" in the Old Testament.

When you come to the New Testament, there's an added meaning for "glory." In addition to the idea of *heaviness* and *weightiness*, the word "glory" also describes *something that carries discernment, judgment, and splendor*. When you combine the Old and New Testament concepts of glory, a very unique meaning develops.

When a congregation enters a time of praise and worship, the glory of God comes. The atmosphere becomes heavy with everything we need, and the glory of God then begins to discern or judge exactly what is needed by each person present. God's glory determines who needs wisdom and direction, who requires healing, and what practical provisions are needed. Then supernaturally, people begin to receive the splendor of what they need from God out of the overwhelming heavy, weight of His glory.

Unity Is the Point of Glory

One of the best examples in Scripture of the glory of God coming upon people is found in Psalm 133:1-3. Within these three verses, God's glorious presence is depicted as the *anointing* that rested on Aaron the priest and the *dew* that descends on Mount Hermon:

> **Behold, how good and how pleasant it is for brethren to dwell together in unity! It is like the precious ointment upon the head, that ran down upon the beard, even Aaron's beard: that went down to the skirts of his garments; as the dew of Hermon, and as the dew that descended upon the mountains of Zion: for there the Lord commanded the blessing, even life for evermore.**

When we worship as a congregation or as individuals, we come into a place of marvelous *unity* with each other and the Spirit of God. His presence then comes, and His glory comes with Him. The exact moment when God's glory arrives and begins discerning and meeting the needs in the congregation is revealed in this passage. It is in the moment of unity that the Lord bestows His blessings.

This passage also describes the moment of God's glory dispersing His blessings as "the dew of Hermon that descended upon the mountains of Zion…." What does *dew* have to do with God's glory? Dew is the moisture that is in the air. It is always present, but it is not seen unless the atmospheric conditions are just right. If the criteria are met, and the air cools enough to reach the *dew point*, suddenly the moisture in the air that was once invisible becomes visible. It begins to appear as droplets of water on everything. Eventually, everything is covered by dew.

David said that when we worship God and get into a place of unity, suddenly we meet the criteria necessary to release the divine "dew" of Heaven. The atmosphere changes, and the anointing or glory of God that is in the air we cannot see, suddenly begins to show up everywhere. The entire church begins to experience a corporate anointing, and everywhere you look, people are being touched by the presence of God. Again, this is the result of meeting the criteria of unity in worship.

Examples of Worship Songs in the New Testament

Written within the pages of the New Testament are a number of worship songs that were sung by the Early Church. Some scholars speculate that it contains as many as 30 songs — especially within the Pauline epistles.

When Paul wrote His letters to the various churches and individuals, he sometimes incorporated all or part of a church hymn. It is as if he was saying, "Hey, I know how I will communicate to you what I'm trying to say. I'll quote the lyrics to that song you all sing in your church services." Ephesians 5:14 is a good example of this hymnic literature. It says, "Wherefore he saith, Awake thou that sleepest, and arise from the dead, and Christ shall give thee light." Those are the words to a real song sung by the Early Church.

Another powerful worship song is found in Colossians 1:15-20. These marvelous verses, celebrate the divinity of Jesus Christ:

> **Who is the image of the invisible God, the firstborn of every creature: For by him were all things created, that are in heaven, and that are in earth, visible and invisible, whether they be thrones, or dominions, or principalities, or powers: all things were created by him, and for him: And he is before all things, and by him all things consist. And he is the head of the body, the church: who is the beginning, the firstborn from the dead; that in all things he might have the preeminence. For it pleased the Father that in him should all fullness dwell; and, having made peace through the blood of his cross, by him to reconcile all things unto himself; by him, I say, whether they be things in earth, or things in heaven.**

Again, these are words to a real song sung by the Early Church. Another song of praise is found in Philippians 2:9 and 10. It declares:

> **Wherefore God also hath highly exalted him, and given him a name which is above every name: That at the name of Jesus every knee should bow, of things in heaven, and things in earth, and things under the earth.**

A fourth song is found in Second Timothy 2:11-13. It says:

> **It is a faithful saying: For if we be dead with him, we shall also live with him: If we suffer, we shall also reign with him: if we deny him, he also will deny us: If we believe not, yet he abideth faithful: he cannot deny himself.**

All four of these passages are actual songs of praise and worship sung by members of the Early Church. New Testament believers expressed their adoration to God anytime, anywhere, in any situation.

Acts 16:25 records, "At midnight Paul and Silas prayed, and sang praises unto God: and the prisoners heard them." These men had been beaten and placed in the stocks within the prison. They desperately needed the presence of God to come. They needed His glory to sit enthroned above them, bringing all of His goodness to meet their needs. So they began to sing, offering God a sacrifice of praise. God was moved, and His glory arrived in the form of an earthquake, which broke their chains and opened the prison doors to set them free.

When you praise and worship God, His glory will begin to manifest and meet your needs.

STUDY QUESTIONS

> **Study to shew thyself approved unto God, a workman that needeth not to be ashamed, rightly dividing the word of truth.**
> **— 2 Timothy 2:15**

One of the most amazing stories demonstrating the power of praise and worship is found in Second Chronicles 20:1-30. King Jehoshaphat was surrounded by the armies of Moab and Ammon with nowhere to turn. Take a few minutes to read this account.

1. In verses 6 through 12, Jehoshaphat prayed openly to the Lord. What did he focus on and emphasize in his prayer?
2. What was God's response to Jehoshaphat and the people of Judah in verses 14 through 17?
3. What happened when Jehoshaphat and the people of Judah took their position in worship (*see* verses 21-26)? What does this story speak to you personally?

PRACTICAL APPLICATION

> **But be ye doers of the word, and not hearers only, deceiving your own selves.**
> **—James 1:22**

1. The worship of God is meant to be a personal, intimate time of connection. Take a moment and describe what your time of worship is normally like. What makes you feel closest to God?
2. Look back over your life. Do you have one or more praise and worship songs that are extra special to you? If so, which ones are they? What makes these songs so unique and help you connect closely with Christ?

LESSON 7

TOPIC
A Passion for Worship — Part 2

SCRIPTURES
1. **Acts 2:46, 47** — And they, continuing daily with one accord in the temple, and breaking bread from house to house, did eat their meat with gladness and singleness of heart, praising God, and having favor with with all the people. And the Lord added to the church daily such as should be saved.
2. **Matthew 26:30; Mark 14:26** — And when they had sung an hymn, they went out into the mount of Olives.
3. **Psalm 22:3** — But thou art holy, O thou that inhabitest the praises of Israel.
4. **Ephesians 5:14** — Wherefore he saith, Awake thou that sleepest, and arise from the dead, and Christ shall give thee light.
5. **Colossians 1:15-20** — Who is the image of the invisible God, the firstborn of every creature: For by him were all things created, that are in heaven, and that are in earth, visible and invisible, whether they be thrones, or dominions, or principalities, or powers: all things were created by him, and for him: And he is before all things, and by him all things consist. And he is the head of the body, the church: who is the beginning, the firstborn from the dead; that in all things he might have the preeminence. For it pleased the Father that in him should all fullness dwell;
6. **Philippians 2:9, 10** — Wherefore God also hath highly exalted him, and given him a name which is above every name: That at the name of

Jesus every knee should bow, of things in heaven, and things in earth, and things under the earth.

7. **2 Timothy 2:11-13** — It is a faithful saying: For if we be dead with him, we shall also live with him: If we suffer, we shall also reign with him: if we deny him, he also will deny us: If we believe not, yet he abideth faithful: he cannot deny himself.
8. **Acts 16:25** (*NKJV*) — But at midnight Paul and Silas were praying and singing hymns to God, and the prisoners were listening to them.
9. **1 Corinthians 14:15** — What is it then? I will pray with the spirit, and I will pray with the understanding also: I will sing with the spirit, and I will sing with the understanding also.
10. **Ephesians 5:19** — Speaking to yourselves in psalms and hymns and spiritual songs, singing and making melody in your heart to the Lord.
11. **Colossians 3:16** — Let the word of Christ dwell in you richly in all wisdom; teaching and admonishing one another in psalms and hymns and spiritual songs, singing with grace in your hearts to the Lord.
12. **Hebrews 2:12** — Saying, I will declare thy name unto my brethren, in the midst of the church will I sing praise unto thee.

GREEK WORDS

1. "worship" — προσκυνέω (*proskuneo*): to worship; to adore; to fall forward upon one's knees and to kiss; it is a depiction of intimate adoration

SYNOPSIS

The Bolshoi Theater, located in the heart of Moscow, Russia, is one of the most important theaters in the entire world. It was built in 1776 by the order of Catherine the Great. Hailed as one of the most significant stages in the world, the Bolshoi Theater is famous for both opera and ballet. In fact, it hosts the largest ballet company in the world. Recently, a large amount of money was invested to completely renovate this theater, making its interior even more magnificent. Today some of the finest music in the world is played on this theater's stage.

God is the creator of music, and He absolutely loves it! Few things touch His heart like the worship of His people. In fact, worship is extremely important in the plan of God. It is an integral part of the Church as well as of individual believers. To be all God has called us to be and to do all He has called us to do, we need a passion for worship in our lives.

The emphasis of this lesson:

Worship is the intimate adoration of God and is a vital part of being a strong, vibrant Christian. When you worship God, His glory is released to meet your needs. He wants you to worship Him freely with your mind and your spirit.

Jesus and the Early Church Were Worshipers

The New Testament Church was *a worshiping Church*! Acts 2:46 and 47 says, "And they, continuing daily with one accord in the temple, and breaking bread from house to house, did eat their meat with gladness and singleness of heart, *praising God*...." Early believers were worshipers from the outset, and all that they were doing, they had learned from Jesus.

Jesus was a worshiper. This is seen in each of the four gospels. The night Jesus was with His disciples in the upper room sharing the Passover meal and Communion, the Bible says, "And when they had *sung an hymn*, they went out into the mount of Olives" (Matthew 26:30; Mark 14:26). Before the greatest time of testing in Jesus' life, He took time to worship the Father, and the disciples took note and joined Him.

Remember, before they were called apostles, Jesus' followers were called "disciples." The word "disciple" is the Greek word *mathetes*, which describes *a student who is totally committed to his master's authority*. The disciples' job was to observe their Master and replicate everything He did. And that's exactly what they did for three years. They were avid *learners*, which is actually a better translation of the word "disciples."

During their time of training under Jesus' leadership, the disciples learned to travel the way Jesus traveled, speak the way He spoke, cast out devils the way Jesus cast out devils, heal the sick the way He healed the sick, and worship the way Jesus worshiped. By the time the New Testament Church began after Christ's resurrection, they were already worshipers — like Jesus — and were teaching new believers how to praise and worship through their own example.

Worship Releases God's Glory

What does the word "worship" mean? "Worship" is the Greek word *proskuneo*, and it means *to adore* or *to fall forward upon one's knees and kiss*. It is the depiction of *intimate adoration*. It literally means *to fall on the knees as an expression of reverence; to prostrate oneself either physically or mentally in front of God to worship or to make supplication*.

When we begin to worship, something amazing happens. God hears us and comes to us with all His glory. Psalm 22:3 declares, "But thou art holy, O thou that inhabitest the praises of Israel." The word "inhabitest" — or "inhabits" — is translated from a Hebrew word that means *to sit enthroned*. This indicates that when we genuinely worship God, He is drawn to us and comes to *sit enthroned on top of our worship*! The environment we create becomes so welcoming to God that He "can't help" but show up and bring His glory with Him!

We discovered in our last lesson that the word "glory" in the Old Testament is a Hebrew word expressing the idea of *heaviness and weight*. The reason for this heaviness is God's presence that comes when He seats Himself atop our praise and worship. As He does, all of His goodness comes with Him! That goodness and glory weigh down the very atmosphere. His presence is saturated with everything good that is needed. Miracles, healings, peace, joy, financial provision, and more are all available.

In the New Testament, the word "glory" also describes the *heaviness and weight* of God's presence, but it also includes the idea of *discernment*, *judgment*, and *splendor*. In this case, when an individual or congregation begins to worship God, He comes and sits enthroned on top of their praise. The fullness of His glory, or the heaviness of His presence, is with Him. In the midst of His glory, the Holy Spirit is present, and He begins immediately to *discern* and *judge* all the needs of those who are present. Out of the splendor of His glory, the Spirit begins meeting each and every one of those needs. All of this happens when you sincerely worship God.

Worship Is Woven Into God's Word

Worship was such an inseparable part of the Christian life that the apostle Paul and other New Testament writers incorporated song lyrics directly into the text of Scripture. Some scholars estimate as many as 30 songs are recorded in the New Testament. There are four specific songs worth noting. The first is found in Ephesians 5:14. Paul, writing to the Ephesians reminded them of these lyrics:

> **Wherefore he saith, Awake thou that sleepest, and arise from the dead, and Christ shall give thee light.**

Apparently, the believers at the church of Ephesus, the largest and most influential church in Asia, were familiar with these words. They had sung them in their church. Paul used these lyrics to communicate truth in a way the Ephesian congregation could easily understand.

In a similar way, Paul wrote song lyrics in Colossians 1:15-20. These wonderful verses describing the divinity of Jesus were actually a song sung by believers in Colossae. Look at the words of this song:

> **Who is the image of the invisible God, the firstborn of every creature: For by him were all things created, that are in heaven, and that are in earth, visible and invisible, whether they be thrones, or dominions, or principalities, or powers: all things were created by him, and for him: And he is before all things, and by him all things consist. And he is the head of the body, the church: who is the beginning, the firstborn from the dead; that in all things he might have the preeminence. For it pleased the Father that in him should all fullness dwell; And, having made peace through the blood of his cross, by him to reconcile all things unto himself; by him, I say, whether they be things in earth, or things in heaven.**

Can you imagine this passage being sung by believers? There is no fluff to be found here — only powerful truth. And Paul worked these words right into his epistle.

He also incorporated worship lyrics in Philippians 2:9 and 10. Addressing the community of believers in the region of Philippi, he wrote:

> **Wherefore God also hath highly exalted him, and given him a name which is above every name: That at the name of Jesus every knee should bow, of things in heaven, and things in earth, and things under the earth.**

Again, this was a song being sung by believers in the Early Church. A fourth passage we can confidently say was a memorable song sung by Christians is found in Second Timothy 2:11-13. It says:

It is a faithful saying: For if we be dead with him, we shall also live with him: If we suffer, we shall also reign with him: if we deny him, he also will deny us: If we believe not, yet he abideth faithful: he cannot deny himself.

What kind of people would sing these kinds of lyrics? Undoubtedly brave people who had a solid understanding of their identity in Christ. Songs like these reflect the mentality of the Early Church. They were brimming with teaching and doctrine, and it showed up in their worship. It is no wonder the Church experienced so many signs and wonders.

God's Glory Was Released in the Midnight Hour

In Acts 16, Paul and Silas had been arrested while ministering in the city of Philippi. After being beaten and placed in stocks in the prison, these two men began worshiping God. Acts 16:25 says, "At midnight Paul and Silas prayed, and sang praises unto God: and the prisoners heard them." Interestingly, when the Bible says they sang "praises," these were not memorized hymns. In this case, the Greek indicates they sang songs that came straight from their hearts to their lips, and the prisoners were listening.

Roman prison cells were deep and isolated, so for the prisoners to be able to hear Paul and Silas, they had to have sung loudly. These men of God needed a miracle. They needed the presence of the Holy Spirit to show up in all His glory. They knew that if they worshiped God, He would come and manifest His glory, and that is exactly what He did. He showed up and shook the prison to its foundations. Their chains fell off, and the prison doors were opened.

What if Paul and Silas had not worshiped? What if they had just sat there and said, "Oh, it's just so pitiful what has happened to us. All we did was obey God in telling others about Jesus. And look where it has gotten us — beaten and thrown into jail!"

If they wouldn't have praised and worshiped God, their deliverance would likely not have come. Paul and Silas knew they needed to bring the presence of God into their situation. So they began worshiping, creating songs with words that emanated straight from their hearts. They were worshiping so loudly that the other prisoners could hear them. And the glory of

God manifested, which was loaded with everything they needed. Out of that glory came an earthquake that shook the prison, and Paul and Silas were set free!

Worship With the Mind and the Spirit

Throughout the New Testament, believers were encouraged to sing praise to and to worship God, using both their mind and their spirit. For example, in First Corinthians 14:15, the apostle Paul said, "…I will pray with the spirit, and I will pray with the understanding also: I will sing with the spirit, and I will sing with the understanding also." God wants us to use our brains and to sing words we understand, and He also wants us to sing straight from of our spirit with words that don't make sense intellectually. Both types of worship have great value.

Paul offered similar instruction in Ephesians 5:19. Again, he stressed the value of worshiping with the mind as well as the spirit. He wrote, "Speaking to yourselves in psalms and hymns and spiritual songs, singing and making melody in your heart to the Lord." The word "hymns" is very similar to the word we just looked at in Acts 16:25. It indicates *composing songs right on the spot — singing straight from the heart.* The phrase "spiritual songs" in Greek refers primarily to *singing in tongues.*

Paul continued saying, "…Singing and making melody in your heart to the Lord" (Ephesians 5:19). The words "making melody" in the Greek means *to pluck the strings of an instrument.* In this case, the strings we are to pluck are those of our own heart. This type of worship brings the glory of God right into the midst of the person who offers it.

Then in Colossians 3:16, we are given a third word of instruction to the two previous directives. Here Paul said, "Let the word of Christ dwell in you richly in all wisdom; *teaching* and *admonishing* one another in psalms and hymns and spiritual songs, singing with grace in your hearts to the Lord."

Notice Paul said we are to "teach" and "admonish" one another through worship. That is, through psalms, hymns, and spiritual songs we are to teach something specific. In other words, music is not just to express feelings — it is also to teach us something about God.

Once a Worshiper, Always a Worshiper

Remember, Jesus was and still is a worshiper. He worshiped the Father while He was here on earth, and He still worships the Father in Heaven. In Hebrews 2:12, He said, "…I will declare thy name unto my brethren, in the midst of the church will I sing praise unto thee." In other words, when we sing and worship God, Jesus joins in and worships along with us!

If you want to experience Jesus' presence moving powerfully among you, begin to worship the Father with psalms, hymns, and spiritual songs. Sing praise with your mind, and sing also with your spirit. Compose songs of worship on the spot with words straight from your heart. Every time you sing, Jesus joins in and sings right in the midst of the Church.

STUDY QUESTIONS

> Study to shew thyself approved unto God, a workman that needeth
> not to be ashamed, rightly dividing the word of truth.
> — 2 Timothy 2:15

1. What is so amazing about God's presence? David had some interesting insights. Read what he said in Psalm 16:11 and 27:4-6 and write your answer.
2. Sing from your heart words of praise and worship to God, and record those words for future times of worship and meditation. Afterward, write out the lyrics of a worship song that is close to your heart and that you love to sing to the Lord.

PRACTICAL APPLICATION

> But be ye doers of the word, and not hearers only,
> deceiving your own selves.
> — James 1:22

1. Can you remember a time when you experienced the glory of God — a time in which you were praising and worshiping God, and the atmosphere of the room became heavy with His presence? Take a few minutes to briefly write down the experience. In that moment, how did God personally impact your life with His glory?
2. In Ephesians 5:19, you're instructed to worship God by "speaking to yourselves in psalms and hymns and spiritual songs, singing and mak-

ing melody in your heart to the Lord." The word "hymns" indicates *composing songs right on the spot — singing straight from the heart.* Close your eyes and begin to think about all the blessings God has provided in your life, including things from which He has protected you. Then, straight from your heart, compose a simple song of thanks and praise to Him.

LESSON 8

TOPIC

A Passion for Prayer

SCRIPTURES

1. **Acts 2:42** — And they continued steadfastly in the apostles' doctrine and fellowship, and in breaking of bread, and in prayers.
2. **Jeremiah 33:3** — Call unto me, and I will answer thee, and shew thee great and mighty things, which thou knowest not.
3. **Colossians 4:2** — Continue in prayer, and watch in the same with thanksgiving.
4. **Ephesians 6:18** — Praying always with all prayer and supplication in the Spirit, and watching thereunto with all perseverance and supplication for all saints.

GREEK WORDS

1. "continue stedfastly" — προσκαρτερέω (*proskartereo*): to persevere consistently; pictures intense focus and hard work; constant diligence and effort that never lets up; it can carry the idea of an addiction
2. "prayer" — προσευχή (*proseuche*): up-front, intimate contact; coming close to express a wish, desire, prayer, or vow; originally used to depict a person who vowed to give something of great value to God in exchange for a favorable answer to prayer; portrays an individual who desires to see his prayer answered so desperately that he is willing to surrender everything he owns in exchange for answered prayer; hence, in this word is the concept of surrender

3. "always" — ἐν παντὶ καιρῷ (*en panti kairo*): at all times; in every season; at every opportunity
4. "all" — πάσης (*pases*): every kind; every type; every sort

SYNOPSIS

Situated in Moscow, Russia is the Novodevichy Convent, a beautiful architectural wonder that has remained virtually untouched since the Seventeenth Century. This magnificently built place of prayer and study was taken away from the Church by Communist authorities in 1922. Seventy-two years later, in 1994, the nuns returned, and it once again became a place of prayer and study that continues to this day.

You will likely never live in a convent. However, that doesn't mean you can't pray. God has called us to pray all the time, in all places, with all manner of prayers. You can pray at home, at work, in your car, while you walk — anywhere. Prayer should be a regular part of your life regardless of where you are.

The emphasis of this lesson:

To be the strong, stable, and mature believer God wants you to be, you need to have a passion for prayer. New Testament believers were *addicted* to prayer, and they prayed all the time. God wants you to pray all the time, wherever you are, about anything you're facing or about anything for which He asks you to pray.

Like Jesus, the Early Church Was *Addicted* to Prayer

Acts 2:42 reveals a great deal about the Early Church. It says, "And they continued steadfastly in the apostles' doctrine and fellowship, and in breaking of bread, and in prayers." We looked at this phrase "continued steadfastly" several lessons ago. It is the Greek word *proskartereo*, which means *to persevere consistently*. It depicts *intense focus and hard work; constant diligence and effort that never lets up*. It can even carry the idea of *an addiction*.

When the Bible says the believers "continued steadfastly," you could translate it as "they were intensely focused, working very hard, consistently diligent, and investing effort that never let up." What was the focus of their intense work and "addiction"? It was the apostle's doctrine, which was the Word of God, fellowship, breaking of bread, and prayers.

Remember, the apostles learned everything about their ministries from Jesus Himself. They were called His "disciples" — the Greek word *mathetes*, which is a technical term describing *a student who is wholly submitted to the authority of his master*. The student's job was to monitor everything his master did and replicate it in his own personal life.

For three years, the disciples walked with Jesus, observing His every action. Little by little, they learned to replicate in their own lives what they saw Him do. They preached like He preached, cast out demons like He cast out demons, healed people the way He healed, and prayed the way He prayed. Their addiction to prayer was learned from watching Jesus. And all that they had learned, *they in turn taught to the Early Church!*

A Prayer Walk Through the Book of Acts

- **Acts 1:13-15**: The disciples were gathered for *prayer* for ten days in the Upper Room. The result of their commitment to prayer was the outpouring of the Holy Spirit on the Day of Pentecost. Acts 2:1 says that as they were gathered for prayer on the Day of Pentecost, the power of the Holy Spirit came, and the Church was birthed.
- **Acts 3:1**: Peter and John were going to the temple at the hour of *prayer*. As they were headed to that place of prayer, they came upon a crippled man at the gate called "Beautiful." The Holy Spirit seized that opportunity, flowing through Peter and John, to miraculously heal the man.
- **Acts 4:24-31**: We see that the believers were gathered together in a house for a time of prayer. Suddenly, as they were praying, the power of God invaded the place so strongly that it shook the entire house where they were gathered. The people were filled with the Holy Spirit and began speaking the Word of God with boldness. This occurrence was birthed during a time of *prayer*.
- **Acts 8:15-17**: The apostles in Jerusalem received word of the Samaritans being saved. Peter and John then went to Samaria to pray that the Samaritans might receive the Baptism in the Holy Spirit. As they laid their hands on them and *prayed*, the Samaritans received this subsequent gift of the Baptism in the Holy Spirit.

- **Acts 9:10-12**: Ananias was *praying*, and God spoke to him. He gave Ananias specific instructions to go to a certain house on Straight Street to pray for Saul of Tarsus. This was a pivotal moment in the life of Saul (soon to be Paul) and in the life of the Church. And it came during a time of prayer.
- **Acts 10:1-6**: God spoke to a Gentile named Cornelius. He was a Roman centurion. Although he was not a Christian, he was a praying man who was deeply devoted. He regularly gave alms, or offerings, and God noticed his devotion. One particular day, an angel appeared to Cornelius while he was *praying*. God informed this man of prayer that Peter was on his way to his house to reveal eternal truth to him.
- **Acts 12:1-12**: Peter had been arrested and placed in prison by King Herod. Meanwhile, the believers had gathered together in the home of John Mark's mother, Barnabas' sister, to *pray* for his release. They were all gathered together in the city of Jerusalem — probably in the same upper room where Jesus served Communion to the disciples and shared His final Passover meal. This was likely the same room where the events of the Day of Pentecost took place. In Acts 12:12, the believers were gathered praying, and while they were praying, God responded. He sent an angel and supernaturally released Peter from prison. All this happened as a result of prayer.
- **Acts 13:2 and 3**: The leaders of Antioch were gathered together *praying* and fasting before the Lord. They were calling unto God, asking Him for wisdom, direction, and blessing. And God answered. He prophetically revealed that He had chosen Paul and Barnabas for a special apostolic ministry. The leaders then prayed and launched Paul and Barnabas on their first missionary journey.
- **Acts 16:25**: In the last lesson, we saw that Paul and Silas had been beaten and thrown into prison for sharing the Gospel. Scripture says, "And at midnight Paul and Silas *prayed*, and sang praises unto God…." They were praying and singing songs when, suddenly, an earthquake shook the prison where they were held (*see* v. 26). A supernatural earthquake, which killed no one, shook the prison, undoing everyone's chains and lifting the door off its hinges so they could go free. Again, this was God's response to prayer.

In all these examples, we see that believers were praying. They were obeying God's command in Jeremiah 33:3, which says, "Call unto me, and I will answer thee, and shew thee great and mighty things, which thou knowest not." They were calling out to God in prayer, and as a result, God answered them and invaded their world. They experienced the manifestation of the power of God.

What Is Prayer?

The word "prayer" is the Greek word *proseuche*. It is the word most often used for "prayer" in the entire New Testament. It is the compound of two words: the word *pros*, which means *to draw very near* or *to be face-to-face*, and the word *euche*, which means *a vow, a wish, or a desire*.

When these two words are compounded, it forms the word *proseuche*. This describes *up-front, intimate contact*. It indicates *coming close to express a wish, desire, prayer, or vow*. Originally, this word was used to depict *a person who vowed to give something of great value to God in exchange for a favorable answer to prayer*. It portrays an individual who desires to see his prayer answered so desperately that he is willing to surrender everything he owns in exchange for answered prayer. Hence, inherent in this word is the concept of surrender.

The best example of this word *proseuche* (prayer) is the story of Hannah in First Samuel 1. Hannah was married to a man named Elkanah, and she had been childless for quite some time. Year after year, she wanted God to give her a child, but she remained barren. Finally, in great bitterness of soul, she came to the altar of God and prayed. She said, "God I desperately want a child. If You'll give me a child, I'll give him back to You. He'll be Yours all the days of his life."

This is a perfect example of the word "prayer" (*proseuche*). Hannah *drew near to God and expressed her wish and deep desire* for a child. With her prayer, she made a vow. She said, "God, if You give me a child, I'll give You something — I'll give him back to You." This is the principle of *surrender*, which is inseparably linked to prayer.

God answered her request. He was waiting for her to come to the altar in a place of total surrender. In that position, she was ready to receive the gift of answered prayer. God opened her womb, and she conceived and gave birth to Samuel, who eventually became a great prophet and judge in Israel.

You may think you are waiting on God to answer your prayer, but it is possible that He is waiting for *you* to come to a place of surrender. Again, the element of coming to the altar to surrender something is almost always involved in answered prayer. If you are willing to surrender yourself to God, He will respond favorably to you.

The early believers were *addicted* to prayer — they were addicted to coming to the altar of God and surrendering their lives. Basically, they prayed, "God, we'll give You everything if You will give us Your power." This was the exchange that took place, and this same exchange is available to you.

How Often Should You Pray?

Ephesians 6:18 lets us know the frequency of our praying. It says, "Praying *always* with all prayer…." The word "always" is the Greek phrase *en panti kairo*, and it means *at all times, in every season, at every opportunity*. A literal translation would read, "Pray in every moment, at any time, whenever you can, whenever you get a chance."

Again, Ephesians 6:18 says, "Praying always with *all* prayer…." The word "all" is the Greek word *pases*, which means *to use every kind of prayer, every type of prayer, every sort of prayer*. When we put all of this together, we get the *RIV* (*Renner's Interpretive Version*) of Ephesians 6:18:

> **Praying in every moment, at any time, whenever you get an opportunity, and doing it with every kind of prayer that is available to use.**

In Colossians 4:2, we are commanded to "Continue in prayer, and watch in the same with thanksgiving." Interestingly, the word "continue" is the same Greek word translated as "continued stedfastly" in Acts 2:42. It carries the idea of *an addiction*. Therefore, when we are told, "Continue in prayer," it really means we are to be *addicted to prayer*. This is the picture of a persistent, never-giving-up type of praying. It depicts a person who wants something so desperately that he prays robust prayers for it. These are prayers that are strong, solid, and *heavy-duty*. It is the picture of serious praying!

So we are to pray all the time, with every chance we get, using every kind of prayer. This lets us know that there are different kinds of prayers. In fact, there are six specific types of prayer found in the New Testament. There is the *prayer of consecration*, the *prayer of petition*, and the *prayer of authority*, which is sometimes called *the prayer of faith*. Additionally, there is the *prayer of thanksgiving*, the *prayer of supplication*, and *the prayer of intercession*.

All of these are kinds of prayer specifically mentioned in the New Testament, and the Early Church was addicted to these.

STUDY QUESTIONS

> Study to shew thyself approved unto God, a workman that needeth not to be ashamed, rightly dividing the word of truth.
> — 2 Timothy 2:15

1. Jesus wants us to pray to the Father and ask for whatever we need in His Name (*see* John 14:13, 14). According to First John 5:14, 15 and John 15:7, what should your prayer requests be filled with? What are you promised as a result?
2. God is ready, willing, and able to answer your prayers. There are certain things, however, that can hinder your prayers. (*See* Psalm 66:18-20; Isaiah 1:15-19; 59:1-3; Matthew 6:14, 15; Mark 11:24, 25; 2 Chronicles 7:14; James 1:6, 7; and 4:1-3.) Look up these verses and identify these causes for unanswered prayer.
3. Are you dealing with any of these issues in your life? If so, which one(s)? What is the Holy Spirit prompting you to do to make things right?

PRACTICAL APPLICATION

> But be ye doers of the word, and not hearers only, deceiving your own selves.
> — James 1:22

1. Look back over your life. Briefly describe at least one major answer to prayer. How did God's coming through for you impact your life? How about the lives of those around you?
2. What are you praying and believing God for right now? Take a moment to share some of the details of your situation. What promises from God's Word can you write down and begin to pray in regard to seeing this prayer answered?

LESSON 9

TOPIC
A Passion for Giving — Part 1

SCRIPTURES

1. **Acts 2:46, 47 (*NLT*)** — They worshiped together at the Temple each day, met in homes for the Lord's Supper, and shared their meals with great joy and generosity — all the while praising God and enjoying the goodwill of all the people. And each day the Lord added to their fellowship those who were being saved.

2. **Acts 4:32-37** — And the multitude of them that believed were of one heart and of one soul: neither said any of them that ought of the things which he possessed was his own; but they had all things common. And with great power gave the apostles witness of the resurrection of the Lord Jesus: and great grace was upon them all. Neither was there any among them that lacked: for as many as were possessors of lands or houses sold them, and brought the prices of the things that were sold, and laid them down at the apostles' feet: and distribution was made unto every man according as he had need. And Joses, who by the apostles was surnamed Barnabas, (which is, being interpreted, The son of consolation,) a Levite, and of the country of Cyprus, having land, sold it, and brought the money, and laid it at the apostles' feet.

3. **Acts 10:38** — How God anointed Jesus of Nazareth with the Holy Ghost and with power: who went about doing good, and healing all that were oppressed of the devil; for God was with him.

4. **Matthew 6:21** — For where your treasure is, there will your heart be also.

5. **2 Samuel 24:24** — And the king said unto Araunah, Nay; but I will surely buy it of thee at a price: neither will I offer burnt offerings unto the Lord my God of that which doth cost me nothing. So David bought the threshingfloor and the oxen for fifty shekels of silver.

6. **2 Chronicles 1:6, 7** — And Solomon went up thither to the brasen altar before the Lord, which was at the tabernacle of the congregation,

and offered a thousand burnt offerings upon it. In that night did God appear unto Solomon, and said unto him, Ask what I shall give thee.

7. **2 Chronicles 7:5, 12** — And king Solomon offered a sacrifice of twenty and two thousand oxen, and an hundred and twenty thousand sheep: so the king and all the people dedicated the house of God. And the Lord appeared to Solomon by night, and said unto him, I have heard thy prayer, and have chosen this place to myself for an house of sacrifice.

8. **Proverbs 3:9** — Honor the Lord with thy substance, and with the firstfruits of all thine increase.

GREEK WORDS

1. "doing good" — εὐεργετέω (*euergeteo*): to do good; depicts a benefactor or philanthropist; one who financially supports charitable works; one who uses his financial resources to meet the needs of disadvantaged people; this word was only used in connection with the provision of food, clothes, or some other commodity associated with physical or material needs

SYNOPSIS

Every week, the Moscow Good News Church is filled with people who have been radically saved by the power of God. They are hungry for the Word and desirous to see the Holy Spirit move mightily. When Russians come to Christ, they describe their experience as "the day when I repented." Their new birth is a powerful turning point in their lives. And once they have surrendered themselves to Jesus, they also begin to worship God freely with their finances.

It is amazing to see their generosity! Not only do Russians open their hearts to Christ, but they open their wallets and pocketbooks too. They believe in the Gospel and zealously do everything within their power to financially see it move forward and transform the lives of others.

The emphasis of this lesson:

Having a passion for generosity is another key ingredient to becoming a strong, stable, mature believer for years to come. Generosity is a major sign that God is actively working in the life of a believer or church. Toward the generous, God behaves Himself generously.

Generosity Began With Jesus

Jesus taught a great deal about giving, and the disciples learned from His example. Again, they were called "disciples," which is the Greek word *mathetes*, meaning *learner*. This word described *a student who is totally sold out and submitted to his master*. His primary function was to learn everything he could from his master and then replicate it in his own personal life.

For three years, the disciples watched and learned from the Lord. Not only did they learn how to pray, worship, heal the sick, and teach and preach the Word, they also learned what it meant to be generous givers. In Acts 10:38, we are given a picture of the generosity of Jesus when it says, "How God anointed Jesus of Nazareth with the Holy Ghost and with power: who went about doing good, and healing all that were oppressed of the devil; for God was with him."

Yes, Jesus went around healing people and setting them free from demonic oppression. But there is something else in this verse that is often overlooked. The phrase "doing good" is translated from the Greek word *euergeteo*, and although it means *to do good*, it also specifically depicts *a benefactor or philanthropist*. This is *one who financially supports charitable works* or *one who uses his financial resources to meet the needs of disadvantaged people*. Interestingly, this word was only used in connection with the provision of food, clothes, or some other commodity associated with physical or material needs.

Therefore, when the Scripture says that Jesus went about "doing good," it specifically indicates that He had an entire segment of His ministry devoted to philanthropy. That is, Jesus functioned as a benefactor, using physical resources to meet the needs of disadvantaged people.

In Matthew 6:21, Jesus made a powerful statement regarding our heart condition and our giving. He said, "For where your treasure is, there will your heart be also." In other words, what we do with our money — how and where we invest it and spend it — paints a picture of what we truly love and value in life. If we truly love our spouse and children, we are going to invest money in their lives. If we love Jesus and His Church, we are going to invest our finances into His Church and His people.

When our hearts are open to the Lord and He is working in our lives, our wallets and purses will also be open. As a result of His generosity with us, we become generous with Him.

This describes the Early Church. They loved the Lord and His people, and therefore freely gave of their treasure.

The Early Church Was a Generous Church

From its inception, the First Century Church was generous. Acts 2:46 and 47 (*NLT*) says, "They worshiped together at the Temple each day, met in homes for the Lord's Supper, and shared their meals with great joy and *generosity* — all the while praising God and enjoying the goodwill of all the people. And each day the Lord added to their fellowship those who were being saved."

This was only the beginning. In Acts 4:32-37, we see that their generosity continued to expand. The Scripture says, "And the multitude of them that believed were of one heart and of one soul: neither said any of them that ought of the things which he possessed was his own; but they had all things common" (v. 32).

Clearly, there was great unity among the believers, which quickly led to generosity. They began to share all of what they had with one another so that no one was in lack. As a result, the Bible says, "With great power gave the apostles witness of the resurrection of the Lord Jesus: and great grace was upon them all" (v. 33).

As the people were generous with their natural possessions, God became more generous with His supernatural blessings. This gave way to even more generosity among believers. Verses 34 and 35 says, "Neither was there any among them that lacked: for as many as were possessors of lands or houses sold them, and brought the prices of the things that were sold, and laid them down at the apostles' feet: and distribution was made unto every man according as he had need."

When we come to verses 36 and 37, we meet "…Joses, who by the apostles was surnamed Barnabas, (which is, being interpreted, The son of consolation,) a Levite, and of the country of Cyprus, having land, sold it, and brought the money, and laid it at the apostles' feet." Barnabas was powerfully touched by God, and he became a very big giver in the church.

Again, hearts that have been touched by God are grateful and open to generously give to others.

Giving Is Inseparably Linked With Sacrifice

During the time of the Old Testament, giving was usually connected to the building of an altar. Altars didn't just miraculously appear. They had to be built. Stones had to be gathered, prepared, and then put in place. When the altar was finally finished, sacrifices would then be offered.

This lets us know that giving in the Old Testament was not a last-minute, haphazard afterthought. It was very well thought out and intentional. Time was needed to plan the constructing of the altar, and resources were needed to worship God through sacrifice.

Take Noah, for example. In Genesis 8:20, we see that he built an altar to the Lord after the flood. He then sacrificed many animals to Him, and as a result, God blessed him and his family.

In Genesis 12:7, Abraham built an altar to God upon entering the land of Canaan. When he saw the giants in the land and the many challenges that were before him, he quickly realized he needed God's presence, so he built an altar and gave Him an offering. Abraham would sacrifice again on this same altar and build other altars to the Lord throughout his life. In response to Abraham's generosity, God was generous toward Abraham and his family.

Decades later, God asked Abraham to give Him his most cherished possession — his only son Isaac (*see* Genesis 22). Without hesitation, Abraham made the three-day journey to the land of Moriah and built an altar to the Lord on the designated mountain. Once God saw Abraham's willingness to give his very best and withhold nothing from Him, God stepped in and provided a ram to be sacrificed in place of Isaac.

Hundreds of years later, King David desired to build an altar to the Lord on the threshing floor of King Araunah the Jebusite. Araunah wanted to give the threshing floor to David along with the oxen and the wood he needed to build the altar and make the sacrifice. But David would not take it. Instead, David said to Araunah, "…Nay; but I will surely buy it of thee at a price: neither will I offer burnt offerings unto the Lord my God of that which doth cost me nothing. So David bought the threshingfloor and the oxen for fifty shekels of silver" (2 Samuel 24:24).

David refused to offer a sacrifice to God that cost him nothing. This is one of the most important principles of giving found in the entire Bible.

Giving is meant to be sacrificial — it is supposed to cost us something. When someone in the Bible built an altar to God, it was usually at a critical moment in his life. That person needed something from God, and it always cost him something as well. As that individual was generous with the Lord, He was generous with them and responded favorably to their offering.

Solomon Gave on a Grand Scale

Without question, David's son Solomon goes down in Biblical history as one of the most generous givers of all-time. At the beginning of his reign over Israel, he went to the tabernacle to seek the face of God and garner His favor. Second Chronicles 1:6 says, "Solomon went up thither to the brasen altar before the Lord, which was at the tabernacle of the congregation, and offered a thousand burnt offerings upon it."

One thousand burn offerings was no small feat, but Solomon desired to make a statement to the Lord! He wanted to demonstrate his great love in a tangible way and implore God's blessings on him and the nation of Israel. According to verse 7, Solomon's sacrifice was well received. Scripture says, "In that night did God appear unto Solomon, and said unto him, Ask what I shall give thee." Whatever Solomon wanted, God agreed to grant it.

Many years later, after the completion of the temple in Jerusalem, the time had finally arrived to offer sacrifices to God and dedicate His house of worship. Remembering God's response when he sacrificed a thousand burnt offerings, Solomon decided to exponentially increase his giving. Second Chronicles 7:5 says, "And king Solomon offered a sacrifice of twenty and two thousand oxen, and an hundred and twenty thousand sheep: so the king and all the people dedicated the house of God."

How was Solomon able to offer thousands upon thousands of sacrifices? It took tremendous planning and preparation. A great amount of time and effort was required to collect and prepare the animals as well as to gather and train the priests. It was a grand sacrifice, indeed, in more ways than one. Solomon was well-organized and very intentional in his giving. There was nothing haphazard about it.

According to Second Chronicles 7:12, we see that Solomon's offering was once again well received. Scripture says, "And the Lord appeared to Solomon by night, and said unto him, I have heard thy prayer, and have chosen this place to myself for an house of sacrifice."

When Solomon was generous with God, God was generous with him. In both cases, God responded to his great sacrifice with great blessing. This is why Solomon's instruction in Proverbs 3:9 and 10 is so valuable to us. He said, "Honor the Lord with thy substance, and with the firstfruits of all thine increase: so shall thy barns be filled with plenty, and thy presses shall burst out with new wine."

If you will honor God with your finances and material possessions, He will honor you and bless you in amazing ways. If you will be generous with Him, He will be generous with you!

STUDY QUESTIONS

> **Study to shew thyself approved unto God, a workman that needeth not to be ashamed, rightly dividing the word of truth.**
> — 2 Timothy 2:15

1. God has much to say about money all throughout His Word. One of the most important verses on the subject is Deuteronomy 8:18. Look up and write out this verse. It reveals the source and purpose of all wealth.
2. Does God determine who gets a *little* blessing and who gets a *big* blessing, or do we have a say in how we are blessed? Read Jesus' words in Luke 6:38 along with Second Corinthians 9:6 and Galatians 6:7 for the answer to this important question.

PRACTICAL APPLICATION

> **But be ye doers of the word, and not hearers only, deceiving your own selves.**
> —James 1:22

1. Jesus said, "For where your treasure is, there will your heart be also" (Matthew 6:21). In other words, what you do with your money reveals where your heart is. A grateful heart that is open to God is generous. Be honest with yourself and with God. What do your finances and your attitude about giving reveal about the condition of your heart?

What do your checking and saving accounts reveal about your love for God and your love for His Church?
2. If you have not been generous in the area of your giving, why? Pause and pray, "Lord, why do I struggle in this area? What am I afraid of? What do I need to do to become more generous like You?" Get quiet and listen. What is the Holy Spirit speaking to you?

LESSON 10

TOPIC

A Passion for Giving — Part 2

SCRIPTURES

1. **Acts 2:46, 47 (NLT)** — They worshiped together at the Temple each day, met in homes for the Lord's Supper, and shared their meals with great joy and generosity — all the while praising God and enjoying the goodwill of all the people. And each day the Lord added to their fellowship those who were being saved.
2. **Acts 10:38** — How God anointed Jesus of Nazareth with the Holy Ghost and with power: who went about doing good, and healing all that were oppressed of the devil; for God was with him.
3. **Matthew 6:21** — For where your treasure is, there will your heart be also.
4. **Malachi 1:7-14** — Ye offer polluted bread upon mine altar; and ye say, Wherein have we polluted thee? In that ye say, The table of the Lord is contemptible. And if ye offer the blind for sacrifice, is it not evil? And if ye offer the lame and sick, is it not evil? Offer it now unto thy governor; will he be pleased with thee, or accept thy person? saith the Lord of hosts. And now, I pray you, beseech God that he will be gracious unto us: this hath been by your means: will he regard your persons? saith the Lord of hosts. Who is there even among you that would shut the doors for nought? neither do ye kindle fire on mine altar for nought. I have no pleasure in you, saith the Lord of hosts, neither will I accept an offering at your hand. For from the rising

of the sun even unto the going down of the same my name shall be great among the Gentiles; and in every place incense shall be offered unto my name, and a pure offering: for my name shall be great among the heathen, saith the Lord of hosts. But ye have profaned it, in that ye say, The table of the Lord is polluted; and the fruit thereof, even his meat, is contemptible. Ye said also, Behold, what a weariness is it! and ye have snuffed at it, saith the Lord of hosts; and ye brought that which was torn, and the lame, and the sick; thus ye brought an offering: should I accept this of your hand? saith the Lord. But cursed be the deceiver, which hath in his flock a male, and voweth, and sacrificeth unto the Lord a corrupt thing: for I am a great King, saith the Lord of hosts, and my name is dreadful among the heathen.

5. **Malachi 3:7-11** — Even from the days of your fathers ye are gone away from mine ordinances, and have not kept them. Return unto me, and I will return unto you, saith the Lord of hosts. But ye said, Wherein shall we return? Will a man rob God? Yet ye have robbed me. But ye say, Wherein have we robbed thee? In tithes and offerings. Ye are cursed with a curse: for ye have robbed me, even this whole nation. Bring ye all the tithes into the storehouse, that there may be meat in mine house, and prove me now herewith, saith the Lord of hosts, if I will not open you the windows of heaven, and pour you out a blessing, that there shall not be room enough to receive it. And I will rebuke the devourer for your sakes, and he shall not destroy the fruits of your ground; neither shall your vine cast her fruit before the time in the field, saith the Lord of hosts.

6. **Luke 21:1-4** — And he looked up, and saw the rich men casting their gifts into the treasury. And he saw also a certain poor widow casting in thither two mites. And he said, Of a truth I say unto you, that this poor widow hath cast in more than they all: For all these have of their abundance cast in unto the offerings of God: but she of her penury hath cast in all the living that she had.

7. **Philippians 4:19** — But my God shall supply all your need according to his riches in glory by Christ Jesus.

GREEK WORDS

1. "doing good" — εὐεργετέω (*euergeteo*): to do good; depicts a benefactor or philanthropist; one who financially supports charitable works; one who uses his financial resources to meet the needs of

disadvantaged people; this word was only used in connection with the provision of food, clothes, or some other commodity associated with physical or material needs

SYNOPSIS

One of the greatest and most encouraging sights to see at the Moscow Good News Church is people surrendering their lives to Jesus. When Russians get saved, they *really* get saved! It is a monumental turning point in their lives. In fact, Russians often refer to their salvation experience as "the moment when I repented."

We find a similar response in the lives of the people who were saved on the Day of Pentecost. In an instant, 3,000 people repented and gave their lives to Christ, and the Lord added to the church from that day forward. Amazingly, all the new believers were totally committed to the teaching and preaching of the Word, to worship, to fellowship, to the breaking of bread, to prayer, and to giving.

The Bible says the people gave so much that they reached a point where there were *no* needy people in the church. Everyone's needs were met because everyone generously gave to the Lord and to one another.

The emphasis of this lesson:

Having a passion for generosity is a key ingredient for becoming a strong, stable, and mature believer. When you faithfully give your tithe and offering, God opens the windows of Heaven and pours out blessings on your life. When you open your hands to give in obedience to Him, God opens His mouth to rebuke the devourer from your life (*see* Malachi 3:11).

Jesus Modeled Generosity

Generosity is one of the major signs that God is working in the life of an individual or a church. The apostles had learned generosity from their firsthand experience with Jesus. They were initially called His "disciples," which in the Greek is the word *mathetes*. Essentially, it means *learner*. The disciples lived in constant fellowship with Jesus for three years — observing and absorbing *what* He did and *how* He did it.

In time, they learned to replicate in their own lives everything Jesus did. They healed people the way Jesus healed. They taught the Word the way Jesus taught. They cast out devils the way He cast out devils, prayed the way He prayed, and worshiped the way He worshiped.

And they were generous the way He was generous.

Of all the topics Jesus talked about in His earthly ministry, money was very high on the list. According to Scripture, there was something to observe in Jesus' ministry concerning the distribution of funds to the needy. In Acts 10:38 it says, "How God anointed Jesus of Nazareth with the Holy Ghost and with power: who went about *doing good*, and healing all that were oppressed of the devil; for God was with him."

In this verse, one phrase often gets overlooked. It is the phrase "doing good," which is the Greek word *euergeteo*. The interesting thing about this word is that it can only be used one way, so there is no way to misinterpret it. "Doing good" (*euergeteo*) depicts *a benefactor or philanthropist*. This is a person who financially supports charitable works or one who uses his financial resources to meet the needs of disadvantaged people.

This word was only used in connection with the provision of food, clothes, or some other commodity associated with physical or material needs. Therefore, in addition to the *supernatural* side of Jesus' ministry — laying hands on the sick, casting out demons, and healing those who were oppressed of the devil — Jesus also had an entire *natural* side of ministry dedicated to philanthropy. That is, He used the finances and resources at His disposal to meet the physical needs of disadvantaged people.

The Early Church Was Generous

What Jesus modeled, the Early Church replicated. Generosity was clearly seen among those early believers. God had touched their lives deeply. As a result, "they worshiped together at the Temple each day, met in homes for the Lord's Supper, and shared their meals with great joy and *generosity* — all the while praising God and enjoying the goodwill of all the people. And each day the Lord added to their fellowship those who were being saved" (Acts 2:46, 47 *NLT*).

The Holy Spirit's work in the people caused them to open their hearts and their pocketbooks and be generous among themselves. They had a heart for the Kingdom of God and freely gave into it to further it in their sphere of influence. People shared their material possessions and even sold their land and gave the money to the apostles to distribute to anyone in need (*see* Acts 4:32-37).

As a result of the generosity of the Early Church, God's supernatural power abounded. That body of believers *overflowed* with signs, wonders, miracles, and salvations. As they were generous with God, God was generous with them. You could tell where their hearts were by observing what they did with their money.

Jesus said plainly, "Where your treasure is, there will your heart be also" (Matthew 6:21). What we do with our money — *where* we spend it, *how* we spend it, and on *whom* we spend it — reveals the condition of our heart. "Just follow the money," and it will tell the truth about what we love and value most in life. When our lives have been truly touched by God, our hearts will be open, and we will be generous with Him and others. This *exactly* describes the Early Church!

A Time When Israel's Heart for Giving Was Wrong

If you want to truly experience the blessings of God in your life in abundance, it is important to know and understand what He said about giving. In the book of Malachi, we read of a time when the people of Israel were not giving as they should, and it showed. Through the prophet Malachi, God said, "Ye offer polluted bread upon mine altar; and ye say, Wherein have we polluted thee? In that ye say, The table of the Lord is contemptible" (Malachi 1:7).

Instead of giving to God with joyful hearts, the people were giving grudgingly. They complained and said, "Oh, it's so hard to give. We just hate to do it." God, who is all-knowing, heard their conversations. He knew their thoughts and told them, "Your heart is wrong about your giving."

God continued His correction in verse 8 saying, "And if ye offer the blind for sacrifice, is it not evil? And if ye offer the lame and sick, is it not evil? Offer it now unto thy governor; will he be pleased with thee, or accept thy person? saith the Lord of hosts."

Basically, God said, "You're bringing Me your blind, lame, and sick animals. That's just wrong. Try bringing those kinds of animals to your governor. Do you think *he* would accept them? Do you think *he* would be pleased with you? I don't think so!"

Then in Malachi 1:10, God said, "Who is there even among you that would shut the doors for nought? Neither do ye kindle fire on mine altar for nought. I have no pleasure in you, saith the Lord of hosts, neither will I accept an offering at your hand." In other words, God told them, "If this is the way you're going to treat Me, I would prefer you stopped offering sacrifices altogether. Just shut the doors to the temple if you're going to dishonor Me so terribly."

Israel Brought a Curse on Themselves

God's rebuke to Israel continued in verses 11 and 12. He declared, "For from the rising of the sun even unto the going down of the same my name shall be great among the Gentiles; and in every place incense shall be offered unto my name, and a pure offering: for my name shall be great among the heathen, saith the Lord of hosts. But ye have profaned it, in that ye say, The table of the Lord is polluted; and the fruit thereof, even his meat, is contemptible."

God was saying, "You who are My people should know better, but you have profaned My name by the polluted sacrifices you're offering Me. Your heart is not right. But My name will be honored and made great among the heathens in the world."

To all this, God added in verse 13: "Ye said also, Behold, what a weariness is it! And ye have snuffed at it, saith the Lord of hosts; and ye brought that which was torn, and the lame, and the sick; thus ye brought an offering: should I accept this of your hand? saith the Lord."

Then in verse 14, God vowed, "But cursed be the deceiver, which hath in his flock a male, and voweth, and sacrificeth unto the Lord a corrupt thing: for I am a great King, saith the Lord of hosts, and my name is dreadful among the heathen."

In essence, God was saying, "You *say* you're bringing Me the best of your flocks, but you're not. Your best is still among your flock. You're actually bringing Me your worst and *calling* it your best. And because of your deception, you are cursed."

God Called Israel To Return to Him

Thankfully, God didn't abandon Israel for her corrupt ways. Instead, He called His people to *return* to Him and do the right thing. He said, "Even from the days of your fathers ye are gone away from mine ordinances, and have not kept them. Return unto me, and I will return unto you, saith the Lord of hosts. But ye said, Wherein shall we return?" (Malachi 3:7).

The people asked God, "How are we to return to You, Lord?" He began His answer to them in verse 8:

> **Will a man rob God? Yet ye have robbed me. But ye say, Wherein have we robbed thee? In tithes and offerings. Ye are cursed with a curse: for ye have robbed me, even this whole nation.**

The people of Israel had robbed God by bringing Him the leftovers and the "rejects" of their flocks. They brought the sick, the lame, and the blind of their herds and kept back the best for themselves. They had robbed God and withheld the choicest sacrifices, and God said, "You are cursed because of it."

Did God need Israel's livestock? Did He need their money? No. He wanted their *hearts*. What they were experiencing was more a spiritual problem than a financial one. Their choice to withhold their tithes and offerings was a manifestation of a spiritual sickness *of the heart*. The only way to make things right was to willingly bring God the money He had asked to be set aside for Him.

Does God need *your* money? No — He wants your heart. Jesus said, "For where your treasure is, there will your heart be also" (Matthew 6:21). When you obey God's command and put your money into His Kingdom, your heart will follow your money. It is truly your heart that God is after.

God Will Open the Windows of Heaven for You

What was the remedy for Israel's calamity for their wrong choices? God spelled it out in Malachi 3:10:

> Bring ye all the tithes into the storehouse, that there may be meat in mine house, and prove me now herewith, saith the Lord of

hosts, if I will not open you the windows of heaven, and pour you out a blessing, that there shall not be room enough to receive it.

God is so gracious and kind. He said, "If you will just do what you are supposed to do — if you will simply bring the tithe and the offering and give it into the Kingdom of God, investing it into the work of the ministry — your heart will be made right again. And when you do, I will open the windows of Heaven and pour out My blessings on you."

The phrase "windows of Heaven" appears in different places throughout the Old Testament. Every time it appears, we see that abundance pours through them. For example, during the days of Noah, God opened the *windows of Heaven*, and rain poured through them without measure. In Malachi, God is saying, "If you will get your heart right and begin doing the right thing with your finances — if you will be generous and give your tithe and offering into My house — your giving will unlock the windows of Heaven, and abundance will begin to pour through them into your life."

Our obedience in giving is the key to the windows of Heaven. When we aren't giving, the windows are closed. However, when we are giving, the windows of Heaven are open, and God's abundance begins to pour into our lives.

What else has God promised to do if we would obediently give our tithe and offerings? In Malachi 3:11, He said, "And I will rebuke the devourer for your sakes, and he shall not destroy the fruits of your ground; neither shall your vine cast her fruit before the time in the field, saith the Lord of hosts."

When you open your hands to give, God opens His mouth to rebuke the devil from your life. For those who give, God says to the devil, "Get away from them now! Move away from their finances, their health, and their relationships. I, the Lord, rebuke you for their sakes." When you open your hand to give, God opens His mouth and begins to rebuke the devourer from your life.

What Was Jesus' Attitude About Giving?

Someone may ask, "Does Jesus really care what I give or how I give? The answer to this question is found in the gospel of Luke. During an offering time at the temple, Jesus was actually observing those who were giving. Luke 21:1 says, "And Jesus looked up, and saw the rich men casting their gifts into the treasury." The word "saw" means *to observe* or *to experience*. Jesus was watching not just what the men gave, but also how they gave. Apparently, the rich men were simply tossing money into the offering out of duty — not in an attitude of reverence or worship. What they gave didn't really cost them anything because they had so much.

Then in verse 2, it says Jesus "…saw also a certain poor widow casting in thither two mites." The Greek rendering of this verse says she was *"reverently putting in two mites."* Although what the widow gave was very small in comparison to what the rich men gave, it was extremely costly to her because she didn't have much. Giving her two mites was a huge sacrifice.

Jesus saw her giving and was impressed by her sacrifice. He said, "…Of a truth I say unto you, that this poor widow hath cast in more than they all: For all these have of their abundance cast in unto the offerings of God: but she of her penury hath cast in all the living that she had" (Luke 21:3, 4). The Greek rendering of verse 3 says, *"What she has put in is more than all their giving combined."* It wasn't the amount that made her offering greater. It was her great sacrifice and the reverent attitude of her heart that impressed the Lord.

When you give with a right heart, it stops Jesus and He takes notice. He celebrates your giving when it is done reverently and sacrificially as an act of worship.

Has God Promised To Supply *Everyone's* Needs?

Many believers often quote and claim the promise of Philippians 4:19: "But my God shall supply all your need according to his riches in glory by Christ Jesus." Although God will meet the needs of His people, the context in which this promise was presented is important.

The apostle Paul was writing to the church of Philippi, who had just sent him an extremely large offering for his ministry work to continue. In response to their sacrificial giving, Paul encouraged them by saying, "My God shall supply all your need according to his riches in glory by Christ Jesus."

Therefore, the promise of God's abundant supply is made to those who willingly and obediently give. Again, when we are generous with God, God is generous with us. If you have not been a giver, why not start today?

Begin by taking baby steps and give *something* to your local church or to a ministry that you believe in. God will honor your faith and begin to bless your life in ways you never dreamed!

STUDY QUESTIONS

> Study to shew thyself approved unto God, a workman that needeth not to be ashamed, rightly dividing the word of truth.
> — 2 Timothy 2:15

1. Carefully read God's words in Malachi 3:6-12. What is the Holy Spirit speaking to you in this passage about *your* giving?
2. Have you ever taken God up on His offer and "tested" Him in the area of giving? If so, what happened? If you haven't "tested" Him in the area of giving, why not try it in faith and watch what He does in response?
3. The Corinthian believers had boasted about promising Paul a huge offering for His ministry. Time had passed, and they failed to make good on their promise. Paul reminded them of what they had said and then encouraged them with the words of Second Corinthians 9:7-11. Read this passage and share how it encourages you to be faithful financially to the work of the Lord.

PRACTICAL APPLICATION

> But be ye doers of the word, and not hearers only, deceiving your own selves.
> — James 1:22

1. Second Corinthians 9:7 says, "…God loveth a cheerful giver." When you give your tithe and offerings, who are you more like — the believers in the Early Church, or the nation of Israel in the days of Malachi? What evidence in your life confirms this?
2. Your obedience in giving is the key to the windows of Heaven. When you aren't giving, the windows are closed. But when you are giving, the windows of Heaven are opened. Would you say the windows of Heaven are *open* or *closed* in your life right now? If they seem to be closed, pause and pray, "Lord, have You asked me to give something that I have not been obedient toward? Have I made a vow that I have

not kept? If so, please remind me so that I might make things right, in Jesus' name."

LESSON 11

TOPIC

A Passion for Holiness

SCRIPTURES

1. **1 Corinthians 6:9-11** — Know ye not that the unrighteous shall not inherit the kingdom of God? Be not deceived: neither fornicators, nor idolaters, nor adulterers, nor effeminate, nor abusers of themselves with mankind, nor thieves, nor covetous, nor drunkards, nor revilers, nor extortioners, shall inherit the kingdom of God. And such were some of you: but ye are washed, but ye are sanctified, but ye are justified in the name of the Lord Jesus, and by the Spirit of our God.
2. **1 Corinthians 6:18** — Flee fornication....
3. **1 Thessalonians 4:3, 4, 7** — For this is the will of God, even your sanctification, that ye should abstain from fornication: that every one of you should know how to possess his vessel in sanctification and honor; for God hath not called us unto uncleanness, but unto holiness.

GREEK WORDS

1. "saints" — ἅγιος (*hagios*): pictures those who are set apart; consecrated; different; holy
2. "fornicators" — πόρνος (*pornos*): encompasses all sexual activity outside of marriage, including both adultery and homosexuality; it is the Greek word for a prostitute
3. "idolaters" — εἰδωλολάτρης (*eidololatres*): the worship and servicing of idols
4. "adulterers" — μοιχός (*moichos*): one who violates another; to take something illegally; to seduce another person's spouse; seducer
5. "effeminate" — μαλακός (*malakos*): pictures men who were used by other men for sexual services

6. "abusers of themselves with mankind" — ἀρσενοκοίτης (*arsenokoites*): male participants in a homosexual encounter or relationship; components of this word describe a man in bed with another man
7. "thieves" — κλέπτης (*kleptes*): pictures a bandit, pickpocket, or thief who is so artful in the way he steals that his exploits of thievery are nearly undetectable; a professional thief; one who takes financial advantage of others
8. "covetous" — πλεονέκτης (*pleonektes*): insatiable desire to have more and more and more
9. "drunkards" — μέθυσος (*methusos*): one who excessively drinks alcohol
10. "revilers" — λοίδορος (*loidoros*): crude; vulgar; pictures abusive language; verbal abuse
11. "extortioners" — ἁρπάζω (*harpadzo*): pictures one who takes from someone else; a scam artist or one who swindles
12. "washed" — ἀπολούω (*apolouo*): to wash thoroughly and completely; points backward in time to a specific moment when this washing occurred; speaks of a definite moment in the past when this washing occurred
13. "sanctified" — ἁγιάζω (*hagiadzo*): to set aside; to consecrate; to make different, holy
14. "justified" — δικαιόω (*dikaioo*): the word for making righteousness
15. "flee" — φεύγω (*pheugo*): to take flight; to run away; to run as fast as possible; it is the picture of one's feet flying as he runs from a situation; to move one's feet as fast as possible
16. "sanctification" — ἁγιασμός (*hagiasmos*): complete separation; holy in practice
17. "abstain" — ἀπέχω (*apecho*): to abstain or withdraw from; to stay away from; to put distance between oneself and something else
18. "know" — οἶδα (*oida*): pictures the idea of developing a skill; to know or remember
19. "honor" — τιμή (*time*): something of value, worth, and worthy of dignity and respect
20. "holiness" — ἁγιασμός (*hagiasmos*): complete separation; holy in practice

SYNOPSIS

One of the oldest streets in the middle of Moscow, Russia, is Arbat Street. It was constructed in the Fifteenth Century, and in the beginning of its existence, it was the home of many wealthy people who were involved in arts and crafts.

In 1812, Napoleon came and invaded Moscow and totally decimated Arbat Street. It was later rebuilt and became the residence of many academics, artists, and politicians. Today, centuries later, it is still widely known for its artisan shops and crafts.

Like many thriving thoroughfares, Arbat Street is always filled with people. On the surface, these people look very much alike, but on the inside, where it's not so easy to observe, there are major differences. For example, the Bible calls us "saints" as believers. In God's view, we are very different — set apart as sanctified for Him and His glory. We are called out from the world to be holy — set apart for *His* purpose to live a life of holiness.

The emphasis of this lesson:

Having a passion for holiness is another key ingredient you need to live a victorious Christian life. You have been washed, sanctified, and justified by the blood of Jesus. You are no longer defined by your past. You are *different*. God calls you righteous, consecrated, and set apart to live by His higher standard of holiness.

Thus far, we have examined six of the ten key ingredients for being a strong, stable, mature believer.

The first is having *a passion for souls*. The second is having *a passion for God's Word*. The third is *a passion for the supernatural working of the Holy Spirit*. The fourth is *a passion for worship*, followed by the fifth, which is *a passion for prayer*. In our last two lessons, we examined *a passion for generosity* — and the seventh essential ingredient for spiritual strength and maturity is having *a passion for holiness*.

What Does It Mean To Be a 'Saint'?

On the surface, human beings look a lot alike. However, as a Christian, you are very different from everyone else in the world. God calls you a "saint." The word "saint" is from the Greek word *hagios*, which describes something *set apart, consecrated, different, or holy*. When God looks at you, that is what He sees — *a saint*. You are not in the same category as unbelievers. You are very different.

Think about the "Holy" Bible. In Greek, it is called *Hagios Biblios*. Of all the millions upon millions of books in the world, there is no other book like the "Holy" Bible. It is in a category all its own. It is *different, set apart,* and *consecrated to God*. There's no other book in the world that compares with it.

The Bible calls us saints (*hagios*), and it is all because of the blood of Jesus. He has washed us clean, set us apart from the rest of the world, consecrated us, and made us holy. God used this same word *hagios* to describe the Corinthian believers in the First Century. In spite of their sordid past, God saw them as holy, set apart, and different.

The Corinthian Believers: *Before* Coming to Christ

In First Corinthians 6:9 and 10, the apostle Paul wrote to the Corinthian church and said, "Know ye not that the unrighteous shall not inherit the kingdom of God? Be not deceived: neither fornicators, nor idolaters, nor adulterers, nor effeminate, nor abusers of themselves with mankind, nor thieves, nor covetous, nor drunkards, nor revilers, nor extortioners, shall inherit the kingdom of God."

Then in verse 11, Paul added, "And such were some of you…." This was his polite but straightforward way of saying, "The list of sinful lifestyles I just rattled off, that is what you all were before you came to Christ." What are the meanings behind each of these words?

For starters, Paul said they were "fornicators." This is the Greek word *pornos*, and it is a word that encompasses *all sexual activity outside of marriage, including both adultery and homosexuality*. It is actually the Greek word for *a prostitute*.

Second, Paul said they were "idolaters." This is the Greek word *eidololatres*, which describes *the worship and servicing of idols*. It means giving oneself to idolatry.

Third, he said they were "adulterers." This is the Greek word *moichos*, which describes *one who violates another; one who takes something illegally that is not his*. The word *moichos* also means *to seduce another person's spouse*.

It is different from "fornicators" in that fornication describes all sexual sin outside of marriage.

Then Paul said that the Corinthians were "effeminate." This is the Greek word *malakos*. It describes *men who were used by other men for sexual services*. In the Greek and Roman world, male prostitution was very common, and in the city of Corinth — which was filled with soldiers and sailors — there would have been widespread male prostitution.

Next, Paul said they were "abusers of themselves with mankind." This is the Greek word *arsenokoites*, and it describes *male participants in a homosexual encounter or relationship*. The components of this word describe *a man in bed with another man*. "Abusers of themselves with mankind" is different from "effeminate" in that it describes those who *willingly* enter into a male homosexual relationship. Again, the city of Corinth would have been filled with this activity.

He then says the Corinthians were "thieves." This is the Greek word *kleptes*, and it describes *a bandit, pickpocket, or thief who is so artful in the way he steals that his exploits of thievery are nearly undetectable*. This is a professional thief who takes financial advantage of others.

"Covetous" is the next category listed by Paul. It is the Greek word *pleonektes*, and it describes *an insatiable desire to have more and more and more. It is greed*. Corinth was a new city, and many people came there to make a quick buck. There were plenty of covetous, greedy people.

Then Paul said they were "drunkards." This is the Greek word *methusos*, and it describes *one who drinks alcohol excessively for the purpose of becoming intoxicated*. Corinth was inundated with alcohol, so drunkards would have been right at home there.

Next, he said they were "revilers." This is the Greek word *loidoros*, and it describes *crude, vulgar, abusive language, or verbal abuse*. With all the other sinful activities running rampant, people using crude and vulgar language would have been common.

Paul ended the list with "extortioners." This is from the Greek word *harpadzo*, and it is *a picture of one who takes from someone else; a scam artist or one who swindles*. Again, extortioners would have been common in Corinth. These scam artists were everywhere taking advantage of people and swindling them out of their money and possessions.

All these types of people made up the membership of the church of Corinth: former fornicators, idolaters, adulterers, effeminate, abusers of themselves with mankind, thieves, covetous, drunkards, revilers, and extortioners.

The Corinthian Believers: *After* Coming to Christ

Thankfully, Paul went on to say, "…But ye are washed, but ye are sanctified, but ye are justified in the name of the Lord Jesus, and by the Spirit of our God" (1 Corinthians 6:11). These men and women who were once wicked sinners had been *changed* by Jesus Christ.

First, Paul said they were "washed." This is the Greek word *apolouo*, and it means *to wash thoroughly and completely*. It points backward in time to a specific, definite moment when this washing occurred. Paul was referring to the moment when the Corinthians genuinely repented of their sins, and the blood of Jesus washed them clean. This word "washed" also carries the idea of *being loosed or set free from something*.

Second, Paul said they were "sanctified," from the root word *hagios*. It means *to set aside; to consecrate or make different; holy*. The moment the Corinthians were washed by blood of Jesus, they were instantly set free from their past. It didn't matter who they had been before. The blood of Jesus — that sanctifying presence of God — instantly and supernaturally separated them from the rest of the world and put them over into a different category. He declared them holy.

Third, Paul said that the Corinthians were "justified." This is the Greek word *dikaioo*, and it is the word for *righteousness*. "Justified" means *to make righteous*. The Greek rendering here literally means, "In one split second, you were declared righteous." The moment they repented, God declared them to be righteous. Righteousness is not what they were *trying* to become — it was who they were in Jesus Christ.

Embrace Your New Identity — 'Flee' and 'Abstain' From Sin

In light of all that God had done for the Corinthians — He had washed, sanctified, and justified them through Jesus — Paul admonished them in First Corinthians 6:18 to "Flee fornication…." The word "flee" is the

Greek word *pheugo*, which means *to take flight, to run away*, or *to run as fast as possible*. It is *the picture of one's feet flying as he runs from a situation*. It carries the idea of *moving one's feet as fast as possible*.

This urgent word of instruction is very similar to what Paul said in First Thessalonians 4:3. "For this is the will of God, even your sanctification, that ye should abstain from fornication." Abstaining from fornication and experiencing sanctification is God's will for your life.

The word "sanctification" is the Greek word *hagiasmos*, which shares the root word *hagios* with the words "saint" and "holiness." It means *complete separation, complete sanctification; to be set apart; holy in practice*. This verse could be translated as, "For this is the will of God, even that you live a separated, sanctified, set apart life." This is the new identity God wants you to embrace.

God also wants you to "abstain from fornication." The word "abstain" is the Greek word *apecho*, which means *to abstain, to withdraw from*, or *to stay away from*. It carries the idea of *putting distance between oneself and things that are wrong*. God wants you to take the practical steps necessary to build a barricade between you and sin so you can't get near it. Specifically, He wants you to put space between you and *fornication* — all sexual activity outside of marriage.

In First Thessalonians 4:4, Paul went on to say, "That every one of you should know how to possess his vessel in sanctification and honour." The phrase "know how to possess his vessel" in the Greek means *knowing how to manage yourself or your being*. The way we are to manage ourselves is in "sanctification and honor." Here again is the word sanctification, which is the Greek word *hagiasmos*, meaning *complete separation, to be set apart, holy in practice*.

God is calling you to live differently than you used to live. He has declared you righteous and holy through the blood of Jesus. He has set you free from everything you used to be in your past. He has raised the bar for living and is calling you to learn the skills you need to manage your body, soul, and spirit in holiness and "honor." The word "honour" in First Thessalonians 4:4 is the Greek word *time*, and it describes *something of value and worth; something worthy of dignity and respect*.

In First Thessalonians 4:7, Paul added, "For God hath not called us unto uncleanness, but unto holiness." Once more, we see the word "holiness" —

the Greek word *hagiasmos*, meaning *complete separation; holy in practice*. Over and over, God reminds us that we are called to live differently. We are to live by His higher standard of holiness. And when we do, the Spirit of God Himself will manifest His strength in our lives.

STUDY QUESTIONS

> **Study to shew thyself approved unto God, a workman that needeth not to be ashamed, rightly dividing the word of truth.**
> — 2 Timothy 2:15

1. Regardless of how you feel or what the enemy says about you, you are no longer defined by your previous lifestyle. God declared you holy and set apart to Him the moment you repented of your sin and invited Jesus to be the Lord of your life. Write out the powerful promises of Second Corinthians 5:17 and 21, which reveal your identity in Christ Jesus.
2. The blood of Jesus is incredibly powerful and is eternally at work in your life and the lives of every believer. The Word of God has much to say about the blood of Jesus (*see* Hebrews 9:11-14, 10:19; 1 Peter 1:18, 19; 1 John 1:7; Revelation 1:5). Read these key verses and identify in writing the power and importance of the blood of Jesus in your life.

PRACTICAL APPLICATION

> **But be ye doers of the word, and not hearers only, deceiving your own selves.**
> — James 1:22

1. Can you remember the moment you were "washed," "sanctified," and "justified" by the blood of Jesus? Can you remember the instant God declared you righteous and wiped away your past? Take a few moments to reflect on the day everything changed in your life and describe what it was like.
2. According to First Thessalonians 4:3, God has called you to "abstain" from sin, which means to *put space between you and the wrong things you used to do*. Stop and think. What sinful behavior have you struggled with in the past or even lately? Pause and pray, "Lord, what practical steps can I take to build a barricade between me and this temptation?" Be still and listen. What is the Holy Spirit speaking to you?

LESSON 12

TOPIC
A Passion for Humility

SCRIPTURES
1. **Acts 2:42** — And they continued steadfastly in the apostles' doctrine and fellowship, and in breaking of bread, and in prayers.
2. **Ezekiel 28:12-17** — …Thus saith the Lord God; Thou sealest up the sum, full of wisdom, and perfect in beauty. Thou hast been in Eden the garden of God; every precious stone was thy covering, the sardius, topaz, and the diamond, the beryl, the onyx, and the jasper, the sapphire, the emerald, and the carbuncle, and gold: the workmanship of thy tabrets and of thy pipes was prepared in thee in the day that thou wast created. Thou art the anointed cherub that covereth; and I have set thee so: thou wast upon the holy mountain of God; thou hast walked up and down in the midst of the stones of fire. Thou wast perfect in thy ways from the day that thou wast created, till iniquity was found in thee. By the multitude of thy merchandise they have filled the midst of thee with violence, and thou hast sinned: therefore I will cast thee as profane out of the mountain of God: and I will destroy thee, O covering cherub, from the midst of the stones of fire. Thine heart was lifted up because of thy beauty, thou hast corrupted thy wisdom by reason of thy brightness, I will cast thee to the ground….
3. **Isaiah 14:12-15** — How art thou fallen from heaven, O Lucifer, son of the morning! How art thou cut down to the ground, which didst weaken the nations! For thou hast said in thine heart, I will ascend into heaven, I will exalt my throne above the stars of God: I will sit also upon the mount of the congregation, in the sides of the north: I will ascend above the heights of the clouds; I will be like the most High. Yet thou shalt be brought down to hell, to the sides of the pit.
4. **1 Corinthians 10:12** — Wherefore let him that thinketh he standeth take heed lest he fall.
5. **James 4:6** — …God resisteth the proud, but giveth grace unto the humble.

6. **Psalm 34:18** — The Lord is nigh unto them that are of a broken heart; and saveth such as be of a contrite spirit.
7. **Psalm 51:17** — The sacrifices of God are a broken spirit: a broken and a contrite heart, O God, thou wilt not despise.
8. **Isaiah 57:15** — …I dwell in the high and holy place, with him also that is of a contrite and humble spirit, to revive the spirit of the humble, and to revive the heart of the contrite ones.
9. **Isaiah 66:2** — …But to this man will I look, even to him that is poor and of a contrite spirit, and trembleth at my word.

GREEK WORDS

1. "proud" — ὑπερήφανος (*huperephanos*): a person who sees himself above the rest of the crowd; one who is arrogant, haughty, or high-and-mighty; one who thinks he is advantaged above others
2. "humble" — ταπεινός (*tapeinos*): pictures one who has become humble; to reduce one's self-importance; to make small; to minimize oneself; to be willing to stoop to any measure that is needed

SYNOPSIS

The Moscow Good News Church is a thriving community of believers. Week after week, people excitedly arrive and eagerly make their way into the main sanctuary. They are hungry to hear God's Word and experience the supernatural working of the Holy Spirit! They have surrendered their lives to Jesus and are submitted to His lordship. Whatever He says, they seek to obey.

This type of surrender and obedience requires *humility*. It is to the humble that God promises to give His grace. He empowers them with His own Spirit to submit to His leading and experience the abundant life of victory through Jesus Christ. Humility is a virtue every believer should desire and acquire in their lives.

The emphasis of this lesson:

Having a passion for humility is a vital ingredient for being a strong, stable, mature believer. God hates pride. Pride is a great eliminator. But He is magnetically attracted to those who walk in humility. Learn to recognize and reject pride and cultivate a heart of humility.

Acts 2:42 says, "And they continued steadfastly in the apostles' doctrine and fellowship, and in breaking of bread, and in prayers." We have learned that the phrase "continued stedfastly" carries the idea of *an addiction*. This indicates that the Early Church was *addicted* to the leadership of the apostles and the sound doctrine they taught. They were totally submitted to their God-given authority. To have this level of commitment, they had to have *humility* in their hearts.

God was attracted to them because of the humility in which they walked. As a result, He consistently manifested His presence in the form of signs, wonders, miracles, healings, and salvations. This is what God desires to do today. But to experience this level of His glory, we must get pride out of the way.

Lucifer: A Picture of Pride

To understand humility, we must also understand pride. Pride is the exact opposite of humility, and God hates it. Even before time began, He has been against pride and has dealt with it swiftly. Such was the case with Lucifer.

The Bible says Lucifer was "the anointed cherub that covers." He was a very high-ranking angel who served in the very presence of God. The name "Lucifer" means *light-bearer*, *light-reflector*, or *one who refracts light*. Scripture says he was covered with every precious stone imaginable. These jewels reflected the radiant light of God's glory. As Lucifer stood in the presence of God, he was like a mirror that reflected God's glory back toward Him. God was able to enjoy His own glory as Lucifer shined in His presence — until pride was found in Lucifer's heart.

Ezekiel 28:12-17 gives us a snapshot of Lucifer's creation and his service near God's throne:

> ...Thus saith the Lord God; Thou sealest up the sum, full of wisdom, and perfect in beauty. Thou hast been in Eden the garden of God; every precious stone was thy covering, the sardius, topaz, and the diamond, the beryl, the onyx, and the jasper, the sapphire, the emerald, and the carbuncle, and gold: the workmanship of thy tabrets and of thy pipes was prepared in thee in the day that thou wast created (vv. 12, 13).

Lucifer was created with all these precious stones to serve as a mirror for God's glory.

> Thou art the anointed cherub that covereth; and I have set thee so: thou wast upon the holy mountain of God; thou hast walked up and down in the midst of the stones of fire. Thou wast perfect in thy ways from the day that thou wast created, till iniquity was found in thee (vv. 14, 15).

Here Lucifer's position is revealed: he was the anointed cherub that covers, serving in the very presence of God. The precious stones that covered him reflected God's glory back toward Him. But when pride entered his heart, everything changed.

> By the multitude of thy merchandise they have filled the midst of thee with violence, and thou hast sinned: therefore I will cast thee as profane out of the mountain of God: and I will destroy thee, O covering cherub, from the midst of the stones of fire. Thine heart was lifted up because of thy beauty, thou hast corrupted thy wisdom by reason of thy brightness: I will cast thee to the ground... (vv. 16, 17).

The iniquity of pride is what led to Lucifer's downfall. His heart was lifted up in pride because of his beauty. As a result of his brightness, his thinking became corrupt and he sinned against God. Isaiah gives us a glimpse of what was going on inside Lucifer's heart and mind. Isaiah 14:12-15 says:

> How art thou fallen from heaven, O Lucifer, son of the morning! how art thou cut down to the ground, which didst weaken the nations! For thou hast said in thine heart, I will ascend into heaven, I will exalt my throne above the stars of God: I will sit also upon the mount of the congregation, in the sides of the north: I will ascend above the heights of the clouds; I will be like the most High. Yet thou shalt be brought down to hell, to the sides of the pit.

Pride utterly deceived Lucifer. He became so impressed with his own beauty and brilliance that he forgot he was just a mirror to reflect God's glory. Pride deluded him into thinking that somehow he was generating his beauty and brightness on his own. Consequently, he became discontent and dissatisfied with His God-given position. He began to think he deserved more honor and more prestige. As his exaggerated opinion of his own self-importance grew, he eventually attempted to exalt himself above God. At that point, God swiftly moved into action and hurled Lucifer out of Heaven.

Pride is an eliminator. It eliminated Lucifer from his God-given position and purpose in the very presence of God. This elimination can also be seen in the lives of people all throughout the Scriptures.

Pride Was the Downfall of Absalom and Judas

In the Old Testament, we read the story of Absalom, one of King David's sons (*see* 2 Samuel 14:25 through 2 Samuel 18:18). He was an extremely handsome and charismatic man like David, but had he not been David's son, no one would have known him. As Lucifer reflected God's glory, so Absalom reflected the glory of his father David.

As a result of David's great fame and influence, Absalom became known and loved throughout Israel. Over time, his good looks and reputation went to his head, and he became lifted up in pride. He lost sight of the fact that he was merely a reflector of his father's glory. He foolishly thought he was better than David and avidly sought to overthrow his own father and take his place as Israel's king. But like Lucifer, pride eliminated Absalom. His life was cut short and his brilliance extinguished.

In the New Testament, we find the story of Judas Iscariot woven throughout the gospels. Judas was in the orbit of Jesus. That is, he reflected Jesus' glory. As a high-ranking member of Jesus' ministry team, he served as the treasurer and handled all the financial decisions. That placed him near Jesus all the time.

Without question, the glory of Christ shone brightly on all those who were close to Him, including Judas. He became highly visible and received much attention. Over time, this went to Judas' head, and he became lifted up in pride. He began to think his wisdom was greater than Jesus' wisdom and attempted to exalt his authority over Him. But pride also eliminated Judas. After betraying the Son of God, he took his own life and, of course, lost everything.

In all three of these individuals — Lucifer, Absalom, and Judas — they were reflecting someone else's glory. Pride blinded them, and they began to think more highly of themselves than they should have. They forgot that they were merely reflectors and began to believe they were generating their wisdom, beauty, and glory on their own. As a result, pride eliminated them. Those who have pride working in their heart will eventually be eliminated.

God Resists the Proud

The Bible clearly reveals that God hates pride. In Proverbs 6:16-19, we find seven things that the Lord hates and that are, in fact, an *abomination* to Him. *Pride* is number one on this list. According to Proverbs 13:10, pride is the root source of all contention and strife. It is no wonder God hates it. James 4:6 says, "…God resisteth the proud…." The word "resisteth" means *to stand against*. Sometimes the resistance one feels is not from the enemy, but rather from God. He is resisting that person because he or she is in pride.

The word "proud" in the Greek is the word *huperephanos*, and it describes *a person who sees himself above the rest of the crowd; one who is arrogant, haughty, or high-and-mighty in his thinking; one who thinks he is advantaged above others*. This is a person who thinks more highly of himself than he should, and if he continues in this vein, he will be eliminated from his position in life.

Pride can be fatal, and you should learn to recognize it, hate it, and avoid it. Do everything you can to get a handle on pride. If you don't get a handle on it, the devil will find it as a handle in your life and grab hold of it. He will use it to manipulate you into doing his dirty work, and because of pride's blinding effect, you will likely be clueless of his influence and control over your life.

Hear and heed God's warning in First Corinthians 10:12: "Wherefore let him that thinketh he standeth take heed lest he fall." It would be wise for you to ask the Lord from time to time to show you if there are any issues of pride in your life that need to be corrected. This simple act of humility could save you from much heartache and even self-destruction.

God Gives Grace to the Humble

Looking again at James 4:6, it says, "…God resisteth the proud, but giveth *grace* unto the humble." While pride repels the presence of God, humility attracts Him. Like a magnet attracts metal, humility in your heart will magnetically attract the presence, power, and favor of God.

The word "humble" in this verse is the Greek word *tapeinos*, and it is *a picture of one who has become humble*. It means *to reduce one's self-importance, to make small, to minimize oneself, to be willing to stoop to any measure that is needed*. This describes a person who has a modest view of himself, not an exaggerated view.

Being humble does not mean you put yourself down or berate yourself internally or in front of others. It simply means you have a modest view of who you are and what you have accomplished.

Always keep in mind that you are never too small for God to use, but you may be too big for God to use. You may be willing to do great things for God, but first He must find you willing to do small things.

What kind of person does God like to use? He reveals it to us in His Word:

- **Psalm 34:18** says, "The Lord is nigh unto them that are of a broken heart; and saveth such as be of a contrite spirit."
- **Psalm 51:17** tells us, "The sacrifices of God are a broken spirit: a broken and a contrite heart, O God, thou wilt not despise."
- **Isaiah 57:15** says, "…I dwell in the high and holy place, with him also that is of a contrite and humble spirit, to revive the spirit of the humble, and to revive the heart of the contrite ones."
- **Isaiah 66:2** says, "…But to this man will I look, even to him that is poor and of a contrite spirit, and trembleth at my word."

All of these verses are talking about our attitude. Being contrite and humble means having a modest opinion of yourself. When you are humble, you attract the presence of God. Walking in humility also sets you out of the devil's reach. In the absence of pride, he cannot get a handle on you. Having a passion for humility will keep you strong, stable, and useful in the Kingdom of God.

STUDY QUESTIONS

> Study to shew thyself approved unto God, a workman that needeth not to be ashamed, rightly dividing the word of truth.
> — 2 Timothy 2:15

1. Learning from the mistakes of others is wise and can keep you from great heartache. Carefully reread the details of Lucifer's downfall. What is the Holy Spirit showing you from his example that you've

not seen before? How does it motivate you with reverential fear to steer clear of pride?
2. The rewards of walking in humility are abundant (*see* Psalm 25:9; Proverbs 11:2; 22:4; 29:23; Matthew 18:4; 23:12; James 4:10). Read these verses from God's Word, and highlight all the blessings connected with humility.
3. How can you learn to walk in humility? Consider Jesus' words in Matthew 11:28-30 along with Paul's instruction in Philippians 2:3-11 for the answer.

PRACTICAL APPLICATION

> But be ye doers of the word, and not hearers only,
> deceiving your own selves.
> —James 1:22

1. Jeremiah 17:9 says that the heart can so deceitful that we can fail to understand what's going on inside it. But God searches our hearts and can reveal to us its true condition. Take a moment to pray: "Lord, are there any issues of pride in my heart? Do I have an exaggerated opinion of myself that I'm unable to see? Please show me." Be still and listen. What is the Holy Spirit revealing to you?
2. Through the apostle Paul, God warns each of us "…not to estimate and think of himself more highly than he ought [not to have an exaggerated opinion of his own importance], but to rate his ability with sober judgment…" (Romans 12:3 *AMPC*). If you have battled with pride, take a moment to pray and make things right with God. "Lord, please forgive me for being prideful and being overly impressed with my abilities and achievements. Create in me a spirit of humility like Jesus. Give me a healthy, balanced view of who I am in Christ. Thank You, Lord. In Jesus' name, amen."

LESSON 13

TOPIC
A Passion for Authority — Part 1

SCRIPTURES
1. **Acts 2:42** — And they continued steadfastly in the apostles' doctrine and fellowship, and in breaking of bread, and in prayers.
2. **1 Corinthians 14:40** — Let all things be done decently and in order.
3. **Amos 3:3** — Can two walk together, except they be agreed?

GREEK WORDS
1. "continued stedfastly" — προσκαρτερέω (*proskartereo*): to persevere consistently; intense focus and hard work; constant diligence and effort that never lets up; it can carry the idea of an addiction

SYNOPSIS
In the heart of Moscow, Russia, is Red Square. For centuries, this historic landmark has stood the test of time. One of the official entrances to Red Square is a highly ornamental gate, and this gate was also once a church. It was originally constructed in 1534, and the gate was built as a church due to a deep, reverential respect people had for church authority. In historical times, people came under the authority of the church as they entered Red Square.

Interestingly, most of the towers of the Kremlin also served as churches for this same reason. Before a person entered the Kremlin, he or she came under the authority of God and His Church. This deep respect for God and for church authority was an integral part of Russian culture.

Similarly, learning to recognize and respect authority is extremely important if you want to make the most of your life and enjoy God's blessings. The Bible says that those who submit to and get along with authority will live a blessed life. Those who rebel against authority will experience greater difficulty.

The emphasis of this lesson:

Having a passion for submitting to authority is a major key to being a strong, stable, mature believer. Submission is vital and central to all of life. As you learn to submit to those God has placed over you, His blessings will be released in your life.

The Early Believers Were Submitted to Authority

Looking at our foundational verse in Acts 2:42, it says, "And they continued steadfastly in the apostles' doctrine and fellowship, and in breaking of bread, and in prayers." We've noted that the phrase "continued stedfastly" is the Greek word *proskartereo*, which means *to persevere consistently*. It describes *intense focus and very hard work*. It indicates *constant diligence and effort that never lets up*. The word *proskartereo* can also carry the idea of *an addiction*. Essentially, the early believers were *addicted* to — very intensely focused — the apostles' doctrine, fellowship, breaking of bread, and prayer. In order for them to be committed to and to receive from the apostles' sound doctrine, they had to be submitted to the apostles' authority, and they were.

Keep in mind, the apostles were originally called Jesus' *disciple*s, from the Greek word *mathetes*, which describes *a student that is completely submitted to the authority of his master*. In this case, the disciples were completely submitted to the authority of Jesus. They did not question His decisions. What He said, they did. The disciples came to understand that submission to spiritual authority and all authority was required in order for them to one day be in authority themselves.

We will cover spiritual authority in detail in our next lesson. In this lesson, our focus is general authority.

Submission to Authority Is Central to All of Life

From the cradle to the grave, submission to authority is *inescapable*. God Himself established authority, and He has done so to ensure things are done "decently and in order" (*see* 1 Corinthians 14:40). In this life, there are multiple kinds of authority we must recognize and submit to:

In the home: Children are to submit to parents, wives are to be in submission to their husbands, and husbands are supposed to be in submission to Christ. (Of course, we are all to be in submission to the Lord.)

In general, people struggle with the issue of submitting to authority. We are all born as rebels at heart. Yes, sometimes husbands have behaved dishonorably, and it is hard for their wives to submit. Likewise, sometimes parents have treated their children harshly, making it difficult for their children to submit to them. But submission to authority is God's system of order and blessing.

One of the very best things we can do for our children, grandchildren, and great grandchildren is to teach them to respect and submit to authority. By doing so, we are actually instructing and equipping them on how to live a good life. Those who learn how to respect and get along with authority are usually the ones who eventually become people in authority themselves. Those who constantly argue with and disrespect authority usually don't get very far in life. In fact, some people's lives are cut short as a result of their rebellion.

In the workplace: Employees are to be in submission to their employers. Workers need to always keep it mind that it is a blessing to have a job. Employers are to be in submission to their bosses or the company owners, and company owners are to be in submission to the rules of law governing businesses.

In the classroom: Students are to be in submission to their teachers and professors. Teachers and professors are to be in submission to the principal or college president, who is to be in submission to the school board or board of education.

In society: Citizens are to be submitted to the authority of the police and governing officials. And the police are to be submitted to the authorities over them. When a citizen disrespects a police officer, there are consequences. Likewise, when a citizen breaks the law, there are penalties to pay.

In government: Senators and congressmen are to be in submission to the president, the parliament, or other higher authorities, depending on the country's form of government. Whatever the case may be, there is an established rule of order and submission in every government. Without it there is chaos and anarchy.

In church: The members and the staff are to be in submission to the pastor. The pastor is the shepherd of the local church who is ultimately responsible for the care of the people's souls. If he has a congregation or leadership team that is rebellious, he cannot lead the church effectively. Rebelling against or undermining the pastor's authority is unprofitable for the people and leaders. When a church is experiencing a lack of submission to spiritual authority, it has reached an impasse and becomes in danger of losing its effectiveness and blessing.

Again, the issue of submission to authority is *inescapable*. It is central to all of life. Those who learn how to submit to and respect authority do well, and those who fail to learn this lesson often pay for it dearly.

Teach Your Children To Respect and Submit to Authority

There are always consequences for failing to submit to authority. Although these consequences vary in nature and intensity, there is usually an inevitable price to pay for rebellion.

A lack of respect for authority in children produces rebellious teenagers and ultimately rebellious adults. Thank God for His grace and His merciful intervention in our lives that can bring wonderful transformation. Nonetheless, disrespectful children usually grow up and become disrespectful adults.

We see this demonstrated in the life of Miriam, Moses' sister. As an adult, she was very disrespectful to Moses' authority. She talked about and criticized him behind his back and to his face. She even tried to manipulate him to get her way. A close look at Scripture reveals that Miriam was not given proper correction by her father. As a child, she was not taught to respect and submit to authority, so she grew up to be an adult who had no reverential fear for authority. It brought on God's stern correction (*see* Numbers 12:1-15).

Don't be afraid to teach your children or grandchildren submission to authority. In fact, as a parent or grandparent, this is your responsibility. You are the boss; therefore to teach the next generations is your responsibility. To instruct and lead and guide those under your care is incumbent upon *you*. You are an authority they should respect, and when you don't teach them to respect authority, you're not helping them. You're actually crippling them. Eventually, not submitting to and respecting authority is going to negatively impact their lives.

Your children or grandchildren are not going to automatically wake up one day and be respectful toward authority. They are born with a rebellious, sin nature. Just as a fish never has to be taught how to swim, children do not have to be taught how to sin. They're born with it in their blood. This is why everyone must be born again and saved from his or her wicked, sinful nature by renewing their mind and submitting to the authority of God's Word. Psalm 58:3 says that from the moment people are born, they immediately go astray. And part of going astray is rebelling against authority.

Therefore, God has called you to train up your children and grandchildren in the way they should go (*see* Proverbs 22:6). Part of this training is teaching them to respect and submit to authority. This training continues right into their teen years. What you teach and model before them about authority when they're young will follow them all the days of their lives. It will affect them on their job, at their church, and in their community. So teach them well so that they can pass on what *they've* learned to the next generation.

Understanding Agreement and Submission

Amos 3:3 says, "Can two walk together, except they be agreed?" The answer is *no* — you can't walk together with someone if you are not in agreement with him or her. It is very difficult to walk together with your boss, your pastor, your spouse, or your parents if you're not in agreement. If you are constantly at odds with them, disagreeing at every step, you are going to get nowhere fast!

The truth is, if you have joined a company, an organization, or a church, *you have actually agreed to be in agreement with them.* The very act of your joining the team communicates that you are agreeing to the team's vision, mission, and methods of business or ministry. By accepting employment or joining a church, you are, in effect, saying, "I agree with and am submitted to your leadership. I am here to help you move your vision forward and fulfill your dream." If you can't believe in and agree with what an organization or a church is doing, then you should not join that team.

There will be times when your employer or supervisor knows things you're not aware of — for example, things about other people's work ethic and details of their personal lives. These are issues he or she is not at liberty to share or divulge. As a result of this information, he or she must make decisions that are in the best interest of the *company*, and those decisions might not always make sense or seem good to you.

Nevertheless, *that person is the leader.* God has placed him or her in authority. That leader sees things not only about people, but also about the direction in which the company or organization is headed months and years down the road. That person in authority sees the "whole pie" — compared to the tiny slice of pie that you're aware of! So in those moments when you don't understand or like the decisions that have been made by those in authority, you must trust that your leader knows what he or she is doing.

Instead of resisting and fighting those who are in authority, why not cover them in prayer? Ask God to help them make the best decisions for all who are involved. Rather than complain about or criticize their leadership, why not get in line with what they are doing and help them advance the vision of the organization or church? God will bless your humble heart of submission.

Dealing With Difficult Authority

You may be thinking, *You don't know how difficult it is to work for my boss.* Or, *You don't understand how hard it is to be in submission to my husband [or parents, or pastor, etc.].* You may be correct — the authority you're under may be very difficult to submit to and be in agreement with. However, God will help you if you will invite Him into your situation. Rather than focus on the failures and shortcomings of others, ask the Holy Spirit to enable you to focus on *yourself* and what He is trying to change in *your* attitude toward authority.

If you have a problem with something that is happening, be respectful about it. Ask for a private meeting with the person in authority in which you can respectfully express your concerns. Most employers are open to and not offended by meeting with their employees. In fact, some are very appreciative that their team members will respectfully and openly share their perspective.

A meeting of this nature may open the door for your leader to explain a few things that you were unaware of that will help you see things in a better light. It may also help you to submit to their authority and keep moving their vision forward.

Revisiting the Example of Judas Iscariot

Interestingly, if you study the life of Judas Iscariot, you will see that he always called Jesus "Teacher." He never called Him "Lord." This reveals a major defect in his relationship with Jesus. Judas was connected with Him for personal gain. He enjoyed all the benefits of being around Jesus, including the amazing anointing on His life and the incredible notoriety it gave him. But Judas never really submitted to the authority of Jesus, and it proved to be a fatal flaw in his character.

Over time, Judas became too familiar with Jesus. As a result, he developed a dissatisfaction with and disrespect for Him that became Judas' undoing. He had opinions about Jesus' leadership — things he simply didn't agree with. Before long, Judas mistakenly began to believe that his own wisdom was superior to Jesus' wisdom — that Jesus should promote Himself politically and declare that He was King. As a result of his improper relationship, Judas ended up betraying Jesus, and he was eliminated from a future of service to Jesus as *truly* King of kings and Lord of all.

A bad attitude toward authority that goes unchecked eventually eliminates people from their spiritual race. Unruly employees who won't submit to their employers ultimately lose their jobs. Church members and leaders who are disrespectful and rebellious toward their pastor will ultimately find themselves removed from ministry. Lucifer, Absalom, and Judas are all examples, as we saw in the last lesson. They were all eliminated from their places of authority because they became proud and rebellious toward their respective leaders.

Don't let this happen to you!

STUDY QUESTIONS

> **Study to shew thyself approved unto God, a workman that needeth not to be ashamed, rightly dividing the word of truth.**
> **— 2 Timothy 2:15**

1. When it comes to understanding authority, it is vital to know and grasp the truth of Romans 13:1 and 2. Take a few moments to meditate on this passage and write what the Holy Spirit reveals to you.
2. The Bible is very clear about how we are to respond to authority (*see* Exodus 22:28; Ecclesiastes 10:20; 1 Timothy 2:1-4; Titus 3:1, 2;

1 Peter 2:13-19). Look up these verses and identify how God wants you to respond to those He has placed over you.

PRACTICAL APPLICATION

> But be ye doers of the word, and not hearers only, deceiving your own selves.
> —James 1:22

1. Be honest. How easy and how pleasurable are you to lead? If you were the leader, would you want to lead someone like you? Briefly give reasons for your answer.
2. After going through this lesson, are their areas in your life where you are *not* in submission to authority? If so, with whom? Take a moment to pray, repenting for any disrespect or rebellion and asking God for His forgiveness.
3. What changes do you sense the Holy Spirit prompting you to make regarding submission to those in authority in your life? How about in the training and teaching of your children or grandchildren?

LESSON 14

TOPIC
A Passion for Authority — Part 2

SCRIPTURES

1. **Acts 2:42** — And they continued steadfastly in the apostles' doctrine and fellowship, and in breaking of bread, and in prayers.
2. **Romans 10:9 (*NLT*)** — If you openly declare that Jesus is Lord and believe in your heart that God raised him from the dead, you will be saved.
3. **John 13:13** — Ye call me Master and Lord: and ye say well; for so I am.
4. **Hebrews 13:7** — Remember them which have the rule over you, who have spoken unto you the word of God: whose faith follow, considering the end of their conversation.

5. **Hebrews 13:17** — Obey them that have the rule over you, and submit yourselves: for they watch for your souls, as they that must give account, that they may do it with joy, and not with grief: for that is unprofitable for you.

GREEK WORDS

1. "continued stedfastly" — **προσκαρτερέω** (*proskartereo*): to persevere consistently; intense focus and hard work; constant diligence and effort that never lets up; it can carry the idea of an addiction
2. "Lord" — **κύριος** (*kurios*): lord or supreme master
3. "rule" — **ἡγέομαι** (*hegeomai*): pictures one who has a leading or visible position; one who has an influencing role in the life of a person or congregation; to account worthy of recognition
4. "follow" — **μιμητής** (*mimetes*): pictures one who imitates; one who replicates what he sees someone else doing; used to describe actors or performing artists who acted on the stage for their profession; the modeling of a parent, teacher, champion, or hero; when a person was known for his high moral character, others were encouraged to follow, emulate or copy that person; implies the intentional study of the deeds, words, actions, and thoughts of another person in order to replicate those attributes in one's own life
5. "considering" — **ἀναθεωρέω** (*anatheoreo*): to fully consider; to analyze; to watch and study; to carefully and fully observe; to earnestly contemplate
6. "end" — **ἔκβασις** (*ekbasis*): the walking out of their lives, their conduct, and their outcome
7. "lives" — **ἀαναστροφή** (*anastrophe*): a word depicting lifestyle; a person's rising up and sitting down; how a person conducts life and how he behaves in every situation; speaks of character, behavior, conduct, and life production
8. "obey" — **ὑπείκω** (*hupeiko*): pictures one who yields to the voice or influence speaking to him; to give way; to yield; to submit
9. "rule" — **ἡγέομαι** (*hegeomai*): pictures one who has a leading or visible position; one who has an influencing role in the life of a person or congregation; to account worthy of recognition
10. "watch" — **ἀγρυπνία** (*agrupnia*): a word that referred to long nights when travelers took turns staying awake to defend themselves against

bandits and robbers who waited to attack in roadside ditches and caves; constant watchfulness, sleeplessness; pictures someone who is constantly mindful about something or someone else; to guard

SYNOPSIS

One of the official entrances to Red Square in Moscow, Russia, is a double-towered gate, which also serves as a church. The reason the gate is also a church is rooted in the cultural precedence that dates back to the Sixteenth Century. At that time, the Russian people were taught that before they could enter Red Square, they had to *come under* the authority of the church. Hence, the people symbolically submitted to church authority by passing through this gate.

History reveals that many of the gates to Red Square were also churches. Entrance into these gates symbolized that a person could not enter Red Square without first coming under the authority of the church. Amazingly, the Russian people had a deep sense of respect for the authority of God and of the church.

Along with the authority of the home, the workplace, and the government, God has also established the *spiritual authority* of His Church. It is vital to recognize and learn to come under this authority in order to be truly successful in life.

The emphasis of this lesson:

Having a passion for spiritual authority is very important if you are to grow and succeed as a believer. First and foremost, Jesus must be the Lord of your life, having absolute authority in all things. Second, you must be submitted to the spiritual authority of the pastor of your local church.

The Early Church Understood Submission to Authority

As believers, submitting to authority is not optional — it is commanded by God. Children are called to submit to their parents, employees are to submit to their employers, citizens are to submit to their government, and believers are to submit to their pastors. First Century believers understood this fully.

Acts 2:42 states, "And they continued stedfastly in the apostles' doctrine and fellowship, and in breaking of bread, and in prayers." The phrase "continued stedfastly" is the Greek word *proskartereo*, which means *to persevere consistently*. It indicates *intense focus, very hard work, constant diligence, and effort that never lets up*. This phrase can also carry the idea of *an addiction*. The early believers were persevering consistently in the apostles' doctrine. They were submitted to their authority and addicted to their leadership.

Where did the early believers get their understanding of spiritual authority? They got it from the apostle, who received it from Jesus. Remember, initially they were called the "disciples" of Christ. "Disciples" is from the Greek word *mathetes*, which describes *a student who is completely submitted to the lordship of his master*. This student never bucked the authority of his teacher. Instead, he replicated everything he saw his teacher do.

For three years, that is what the disciples did. They walked with Jesus and went everywhere He went. They observed everything He did and then replicated it in their own lives. They called Him *Master* and they called Him *Lord*.

If you study the gospels, you will never see the disciples call Jesus, "Jesus." Instead, they called Him "Master" and "Lord." Jesus confirms this in John 13:13. He said, "Ye call me Master and Lord: and ye say well; for so I am." Jesus didn't argue or debate His identity. He simply commended them for calling Him who He is — *Master* and *Lord*.

The Lordship of Christ

The Christian life begins with submission to Christ's absolute authority in our lives. This means He is Lord. Many people come to Jesus and call Him *Savior*, but they don't call Him *Lord*. There is a major problem with this because the Bible tells us in Romans 10:9 (*NLT*), "If you confess with your mouth that *Jesus is Lord* and believe in your heart that God raised him from the dead, you will be saved."

There are many who say, "Well, I believe Jesus was raised from the dead, and therefore, I'm saved." However, they have overlooked the first part of the verse, which says you have to call Jesus "Lord." The lordship of Christ is essential for a person to become born again. That's what God's Word says, and it cannot be ignored.

The word "Lord" is the Greek word *kurios*, and its meaning is undeniable. It describes *a lord or one who is a supreme master*, and inherent in the word "lord" is the idea of *submission*. Therefore, when a person comes to Christ and says, "Jesus is Lord," he is saying, "Jesus, You have become the Supreme Master of my life. You are the one with absolute authority. From this moment forward, I am in complete submission to You. You are the one who calls the shots in my life." This is what we mean every time we call Jesus "Lord."

As Lord, Jesus does not have to ask us our opinion or for permission to do anything in our lives. He is the Lord. We are the student — the disciple (*mathetes*). There will be times when we appreciate what Jesus is asking us to do, and there will be times when we *won't* necessarily appreciate what He is asking us to do. Regardless of whether we like it or not, He is Lord — and as Lord, He has absolute authority to tell us what to do. Our job is to say, "Yes Sir."

Realize that as Lord, Jesus knows what you don't know and sees what you don't see. He only has your best interest in mind. If you buck His authority, you are making it more difficult for Him to lead you and bless your life.

Correct Terminology Is Important

You have a natural, earthly father and mother. You do not call them by their first names. You call them by the unique title of endearment they hold. You call your dad, "Dad," "Daddy," or "Father." Likewise, you call your mom, "Mom," "Mama," or "Mother." There is usually no other person in the world you call "Daddy" or "Mama."

Furthermore, every time you call your dad, "Daddy," you recognize who *you are* and who *he is* in your life. He is your father, and you are his son or daughter. The term "daddy" defines your relationship. Similarly, every time you call your mom, "Mama," you recognize who *she is* and who *you are*. She is your mother, and you are her son or daughter. Correct terminology is very important.

When it comes to spiritual authority, there is only one person in your life that you can call "pastor." Now out of respect, you may refer to someone else as "Pastor So-and-so," but there is really only one pastor in your life. Every time you call your pastor by his title, "Pastor," you are recognizing him or her as the man or woman who has spiritual authority in your life.

And in a spiritual sense, you are submitting to your pastor's authority by addressing him as such.

Correct terminology is extremely important. You only have one pastor, and no one else should hold that position in your life.

Study and Really Get To Know Your Pastor

Once you know who your God-given pastor is, the instructions of Hebrews 13:7 become quite significant for you. It says, "Remember them which have the rule over you, who have spoken unto you the word of God: whose faith follow, considering the end of their conversation [lives]."

First, it says, "Remember them which have the *rule* over you...." The word "rule" is the Greek word *hegeomai*, and it describes *one who has a leading or visible position; one who has an influencing role in the life of a person or congregation*. It also means *to account one worthy of recognition*. Therefore, the one who "rules" over you as your pastor should be a person who has a visible or leading position. He or she should have an influencing role in your life and a role worthy of recognition.

Next, it says, "...Whose faith *follow*...." The word "follow" is the Greek word *mimetes*, which means *one who imitates* or *one who replicates what he sees someone else doing*. The word *mimetes* was used to describe *actors or performing artists who acted on the stage for their profession*. It was also used to depict *the modeling of a parent, teacher, champion, or hero*. For instance, when a person was known for his high moral character, others were encouraged to follow, emulate, or copy that person. Thus, the word *mimetes* implies *the intentional study of the deeds, words, actions, and thoughts of another person in order to replicate those attributes in one's own life*.

When the Bible says, "...Whose faith *follow*...," it is telling us to look at the faith of our leaders and do everything we can to replicate their high, moral character. We are to study them — their thoughts, words, and actions — and duplicate the attributes of their lives in our own lives.

Hebrews 13:7 goes on to say, "...Whose faith follow, *considering* the end of their conversation [lives]." The word "considering" is the Greek word *anatheoreo*, and it means *to fully consider, analyze, watch, or study; earnestly contemplate; carefully observe*.

What are we to fully consider, analyze, watch and study? It says, "the *end* of their lives." The word "end" is the Greek word *ekbasis*, and it literally means *the walking out of their lives*. It describes *their conduct and their outcome*. The word "lives," or "conversation" in the *King James Version*, is the Greek word *anastrophe*, which is a word depicting *a person's lifestyle, a person's rising up and sitting down, or how a person conducts his life and behaves in every situation*. The word *anastrophe* speaks of *character, behavior, conduct, and life production*.

Putting all this together, Hebrews 13:7 says that pastors should have a visible, leading position and an influencing role in your life. You are to "follow" their faith — that is, you are to study their character and their faith and see how they live. You are to fully observe and analyze their lives, considering their rising up, their going in and out, their handling of each situation they face, and the end outcome of their lives. You are to contemplate the total picture of their existence and make it your aim to replicate their attributes in your own life.

Submit and Yield to Their Leadership

Hebrews 13:17 gives us additional direction concerning our relationship with spiritual authority. It says, "Obey them that have the rule over you, and submit yourselves: for they watch for your souls, as they that must give account, that they may do it with joy, and not with grief: for that is unprofitable for you."

First, you are instructed to "*obey* them that *rule* over you…." The word "obey" is the Greek word *hupeiko*, which indicates *one who yields to the voice or influence speaking to him*; *to give way, to yield*, or *to submit*. The word "rule" is the Greek word *hegeomai*, and it pictures *one who has the leading, visible spiritual role in your life*. To "obey" your pastor means you acknowledge he has more authority and possibly more experience than you. To replicate the fruit you see in his life, you will likely have to yield your life to his and begin saying what he says and doing what he does. This is a picture of yielding in submission to authority.

The verse goes on to say, "…Submit yourselves: for they *watch* for your souls…." The word "watch" is the Greek word *agrupnia* — a term that referred to *long nights when travelers took turns staying awake to defend themselves against bandits and robbers who waited to attack in roadside ditches and caves*. It depicts *constant watchfulness and even sleeplessness; someone who is constantly mindful about something or someone else*. This word "watch" (*agrupnia*) perfectly pictures the role of a pastor.

Good pastors, even when they take vacations, are never totally away from their ministry. They have to be available at all times. If someone has a crisis, and no one else can step in to handle it, they have to take the phone call or even come home and deal with the situation. They are the pastor, and there's a kind of a "sleeplessness" — a call to constantly being on guard — that goes with the territory.

So by all means, pray for your pastor! It is in your best interest to undergird him in your faith and prayers.

Realize There Is No Perfect Pastor

Please understand that there is no such thing as perfect sheep, a perfect church, or a perfect pastor. You'll never find them. Looking for perfection will always leave you disappointed and hopeless. Therefore, when choosing a pastor or spiritual leader, look for someone who has fruit in his life that you want to replicate in your own life. Search for someone whose character, faith, and conduct is what you want to see in yourself and in your children and grandchildren.

Ultimately, you should only be in a church where you respect the leader. The pastor's faith should inspire you and be something you want to follow and imitate. You should never be in a church where you have no respect for the pastor. The person you call "pastor" should be someone whose voice you are willing to listen to and whose example you are willing to follow and duplicate, considering the final outcomes, or the fruitfulness, of his life.

A good pastor or spiritual leader is one who understands the seriousness of the responsibility to which he has been called. That person has a reverential fear of the Lord, knowing that he will give account for how he pastored you.

Realize that you cannot bypass submission to spiritual authority and expect to succeed in life. Once you come into alignment with and submission to the spiritual authority God has ordained for you, a conduit will be established through which great blessings will begin to flow into your life.

STUDY QUESTIONS

> Study to shew thyself approved unto God, a workman that needeth not to be ashamed, rightly dividing the word of truth.
> — 2 Timothy 2:15

1. Spiritual authority is powerful and important! Take a few moments to carefully read these verses: Luke 10:19; Matthew 16:19, 18:19, 28:18-20; and John 20:23. Identify *where* spiritual authority comes from and *what* it looks like.
2. There may be times when the spiritual authority we are under becomes corrupt. David experienced this firsthand as he served under King Saul. Read the account in First Samuel 24:1-15 of when David had the opportunity to strike out against Saul's ungodly treatment, but he chose to refrain. What can you learn from David's example and apply in your own life?

PRACTICAL APPLICATION

> But be ye doers of the word, and not hearers only, deceiving your own selves.
> — James 1:22

1. In First Timothy 2:1-3, God instructs us to pray for all those in leadership, which includes our pastors. Do you pray for your pastor and his family? If so, what type of things do you pray for them and how often do you lift them up in prayer?
2. Take a few moments right now to *thank God* for your pastor and express your appreciation for the positive impact he has made on your life. Then pray for him and his family in the same way you would want someone to pray for you and your family.
3. This week, consider picking up a greeting card for your pastor and his family. Take a few moments to express your thanks for his positive influence on your life — allowing other family members to share their appreciation too, if they would like. Also consider including a gift card to a favorite restaurant as a way of saying *thanks*.

LESSON 15

TOPIC
A Passion for the Fear of the Lord

SCRIPTURES
1. **Proverbs 9:10** — The fear of the Lord is the beginning of wisdom: and the knowledge of the holy is understanding.
2. **Acts 2:42, 43** — And they continued stedfastly in the apostles' doctrine and fellowship, and in breaking of bread, and in prayers. And fear came upon every soul: and many wonders and signs were done by the apostles.
3. **Acts 4:32-37** — And the multitude of them that believed were of one heart and of one soul: neither said any of them that ought of the things which he possessed was his own; but they had all things common. And with great power gave the apostles witness of the resurrection of the Lord Jesus: and great grace was upon them all. Neither was there any among them that lacked: for as many as were possessors of lands or houses sold them, and brought the prices of the things that were sold, and laid them down at the apostles' feet: and distribution was made unto every man according as he had need. And Joses, who by the apostles was surnamed Barnabas, (which is, being interpreted, The son of consolation,) a Levite, and of the country of Cyprus, having land, sold it, and brought the money, and laid it at the apostles' feet.
4. **Acts 5:1-11** — But a certain man named Ananias, with Sapphira his wife, sold a possession, And kept back part of the price, his wife also being privy to it, and brought a certain part, and laid it at the apostles' feet. But Peter said, Ananias, why hath Satan filled thine heart to lie to the Holy Ghost, and to keep back part of the price of the land? Whiles it remained, was it not thine own? and after it was sold, was it not in thine own power? why hast thou conceived this thing in thine heart? thou hast not lied unto men, but unto God. And Ananias hearing these words fell down, and gave up the ghost: and great fear came on all them that heard these things. And the young men arose, wound him up, and carried him out, and buried him.

And it was about the space of three hours after, when his wife, not knowing what was done, came in. And Peter answered unto her, Tell me whether ye sold the land for so much? And she said, Yea, for so much. Then Peter said unto her, How is it that ye have agreed together to tempt the Spirit of the Lord? behold, the feet of them which have buried thy husband are at the door, and shall carry thee out. Then fell she down straightway at his feet, and yielded up the ghost: and the young men came in, and found her dead, and, carrying her forth, buried her by her husband. And great fear came upon all the church, and upon as many as heard these things.

GREEK WORDS

1. "lie" — ψεύδομαι (*pseudomai*): to lie; to deceive; to willfully falsify or misrepresent facts
2. "conceived" — τίθημι (*tithemi*): to set in place; to set in position; to conceive a plan
3. "thing" — πρᾶγμα (*pragma*): an action or affair; a well-conceived deed
4. "to God" — Θεῷ (*Theo*): Literally, "to God," making it clear that the Holy Spirit is God
5. "fear" — φόβος (*phobos*): alarm; hush, amazement, or respect; usually depicts a fear that results from a threatening or alarming circumstance
6. "agreed together" — συμφωνέω (*sumphoneo*): to be in harmony; it is the word from which "symphony" is derived
7. "all" — ὅλος (*holos*): whole; entire; complete

SYNOPSIS

In 1897, the very first thermal power plant opened in Russia just across the river from the Kremlin. It is called Power Station Number One, and it has provided electricity to homes, hospitals, schools, apartments, and buildings of all kinds for more than 120 years. It is still in operation today.

Life would be very different without electricity. It is extremely important and valuable, but it must be respected. Just as it has the power to help you, it also has the power to hurt you if it is mishandled. We need to have a healthy respect for electricity.

In the same way, we need to have a healthy respect for the power of God. In fact, we need to have a healthy *fear of the Lord*. Just as His power can give life, it can also have disastrous, negative effects if mishandled, as we will clearly see in this lesson.

Here is a quick recap of the ten essential ingredients you need to be a strong, stable, mature believer for years to come.

1. Passion for souls
2. Passion for God's Word
3. Passion for the supernatural work of the Holy Spirit
4. Passion for worship
5. Passion for prayer
6. Passion for generosity
7. Passion for holiness
8. Passion for humility
9. Passion for authority

And number ten is *a passion for the fear of the Lord.*

The emphasis of this lesson:

Having a passion for the fear of the Lord is having a deep reverence, respect, awe, and healthy fear for who He is. The power of the Holy Spirit will bring life-giving blessings when respected and handled correctly. If we lack the fear of the Lord by mishandling or disrespecting His presence and power, we will experience negative consequences.

What Is the Fear of the Lord?

Not many people talk about the fear of the Lord. As a matter of fact, many Christians are confused about what it is. Some believers quote Second Timothy 1:7, which says, "For God hath not given us the spirit of fear…" and mistakenly claim that the fear of the Lord is not biblical. However, the fear of the Lord *is* biblical and, in fact, foundational to the Christian faith.

What is the fear of the Lord? First consider the difference between fear and respect in the following illustrations:

Making Wrong Choices — Life has consequences. If you break the law or violate the rules, you will suffer the "side effect" or consequences. Does this mean that you should be afraid of rules and laws? No. It simply means you should respect and obey them.

Disrespecting Your Employer — If you disrespect and fail to submit to your employer, there will be consequences. Does this mean you should be afraid of your employer? No. It simply means you should respect and submit to his or her authority.

Dishonoring the Police — If you dishonor and disregard the authority of the police, you will likely experience negative consequences. No one says, "The police love you and are *only* around you to bless you. You never need to fear them." The truth is, if you break the law, the same police who are there to serve and protect you are the same police who will quickly arrest you! Does this mean you should be afraid of the police? No. It simply means you should honor and respect their authority.

Mishandling Electricity — If you mishandle electricity, you will suffer the consequences. Electricity is meant to bring life and enhance your daily existence. However, what electricity produces depends on how it is handled. If you handle it correctly, it will be a blessing. If you mishandle it, it can kill you. Does this mean you should be afraid of electricity? No. It simply means you should have a healthy respect for it and handle it properly.

The fear of the Lord is much the same. If you mishandle the power and presence of God, you will suffer negative consequences. However, if you respectfully and honorably handle His power and presence, it will produce amazing blessings in your life. The fear of the Lord does not mean to be afraid of Him. It means to have a deep reverence, respect, awe, and healthy fear of who He is.

Proverbs 9:10 says, "The fear of the Lord is the beginning of wisdom: and the knowledge of the holy is understanding." The starting point of wisdom is to fear the Lord. Your attitude toward God, His power, and the supernatural work of His Holy Spirit will determine what the Spirit produces in your life.

Early Believers Feared the Lord

First Century believers learned to have a healthy, reverential fear of the Lord very early. Acts 2:42 and 43 says, "And they continued steadfastly in the apostles' doctrine and fellowship, and in breaking of bread, and in prayers. And *fear* came upon every soul: and many wonders and signs were done by the apostles." This "fear" that came on every soul was a reverential fear for the power of God. They respected what He was doing among them, and where God's power is respected, God's Spirit brings great benefit to the church and to individuals.

The fear of the Lord among believers produced "many wonders and signs." We see this not only in Acts 2, but also in Acts 4. It says, "And the multitude of them that believed were of one heart and of one soul: neither said any of them that ought of the things which he possessed was his own; but they had all things common" (v. 32). God had moved on their hearts, and they became very generous with each other and with Him. As they were generous with God, God was generous with them.

Verses 33-35 says, "And with great power gave the apostles witness of the resurrection of the Lord Jesus: and great grace was upon them all. Neither was there any among them that lacked: for as many as were possessors of lands or houses sold them, and brought the prices of the things that were sold, and laid them down at the apostles' feet: and distribution was made unto every man according as he had need."

The cycle of generous giving to God and one another, followed by the supernatural signs and wonders of the Holy Spirit's power, continued to build. Then in Acts 4:36 and 37, we read that something amazing happened. Scripture says, "And Joses, who by the apostles was surnamed Barnabas, (which is, being interpreted, The son of consolation,) a Levite, and of the country of Cyprus, having land, sold it, and brought the money, and laid it at the apostles' feet."

This man named Joses had been saved by God, and he became so overwhelmingly grateful for the transforming work of the Holy Spirit in his life, he just had to do something in response. So he sold some land he had, and it yielded what appears to be a significant sum of money. Joses then brought all the proceeds and laid them at the apostles' feet. His offering generated so much encouragement among the early believers that they said, "Man! This guy is such an encouragement to us! We're not going to call him Joses anymore. We're going to call him Barnabas, meaning *son of encouragement*."

Undoubtedly, many people in the church witnessed this huge, sacrificial gift made by Barnabas. They also witnessed how the other believers celebrated him. Among the onlookers was a couple named Ananias and his wife Sapphira.

A Powerful Lesson From the Lives of Ananias and Sapphira

After observing the appreciation expressed to Barnabas, Ananias and Sapphira decided to sell a piece of their land and give some of the proceeds to the church. Apparently, they saw it as a way to elevate themselves in the eyes of the people and possibly receive a promotion into a place of leadership. They acted out of impure motivation and a lack of the fear of the Lord. Their story is recorded in Acts 5:1-11:

> **But a certain man named Ananias, with Sapphira his wife, sold a possession, and kept back part of the price, his wife also being privy to it, and brought a certain part, and laid it at the apostles' feet" (vv. 1, 2).**

There was nothing wrong with them selling the land and keeping a part of the profit for themselves. It was their land, and they could give what they wanted to give and keep what they wanted to keep. What they did wrong was that they lied about what they actually did.

Verse 3 records, "But Peter said, Ananias, why hath Satan filled thine heart to *lie* to the Holy Ghost, and to keep back part of the price of the land?" The word "lie" is the Greek word *pseudomai*, which means *to lie, to deceive, to willfully falsify,* or *to misrepresent the facts*. Ananias' actions were a willful misrepresentation of the truth, and that is what Peter rebuked him for in verse 3.

Then in verse 4, Peter further said:

> **Whiles it remained, was it not thine own? And after it was sold, was it not in thine own power? Why hast thou conceived this thing in thine heart? Thou hast not lied unto men, but unto God.**

The word "conceived" is the Greek word *tithemi*, which means *to set something in place, to set something in position,* or *to conceive a plan*. The word "thing" is the Greek word *pragma*, which would be better translated as *an action, an affair,* or a *well-conceived deed*. These two words confirm that Ananias and Sapphira had a premeditated strategy they were working out.

Notice what Peter said in verse 3: "Why hath Satan filled thine heart to lie to the Holy Ghost...?" Then in the very next verse, he said, "Thou hast not lied unto men, but unto God." These two statements taken together revealed a powerful truth to the Early Church: *The Holy Spirit is not just a fragmented representation of God; the Holy Spirit is God in the Church. And how you treat the Holy Spirit is how you treat God.*

Verse 5 reveals a very powerful lesson to the early believers:

> **And Ananias hearing these words fell down, and gave up the ghost: and great fear came on all them that heard these things.**

Right before the eyes of the Early Church, and recorded for believers of all generations, is what can happen when we mishandle the power and presence of the Holy Spirit. Ananias died, and great fear came on the people who saw it and heard about it. The word "great" is the word *mega*, and it describes *something enormous and all-consuming*. The word "fear" is the word *phobos*, and it describes *terror, alarm, hush, amazement, or respect*. It usually depicts *a fear that results from a threatening or an alarming circumstance.*

The instant Ananias died, an enormous, all-consuming fear came upon the early believers. That is, *a fear, a hush, an amazement, a trembling* literally came upon the entire church.

The story continues in verses 6-9:

> **And the young men arose, wound him up, and carried him out, and buried him. And it was about the space of three hours after, when his wife, not knowing what was done, came in. And Peter answered unto her, Tell me whether ye sold the land for so much? And she said, Yea, for so much. Then Peter said unto her, How is it that ye have agreed together to tempt the Spirit of the Lord? Behold, the feet of them which have buried thy husband are at the door, and shall carry thee out.**

Sapphira had the opportunity to tell the truth, but she didn't. She carried out the strategy she and Ananias had conceived — to make the apostles and church members believe they had given all the proceeds from the sale of the land. Peter then said, "How is it that ye have *agreed together* to tempt the Spirit of the Lord?" The phrase "agreed together" is the Greek word *sumphoneo*, and it means *to be in harmony*. It is the word from which *symphony* is derived. Ananias and Sapphira harmonized their thoughts, words, and actions in a concerted effort to falsify the facts. But their plan did not succeed. Verses 10 and 11 reveal Sapphira's fate and the people's response:

> **Then fell she down straightway at his feet, and yielded up the ghost: and the young men came in, and found her dead, and, carrying her forth, buried her by her husband. And great fear came upon all the church, and upon as many as heard these things.**

A second time it is said that "great fear came upon all the church…." The word "great" is again the Greek word *mega*, meaning *something enormous and all-encompassing*. Likewise, the word "fear" is the same Greek word for fear in verse 5 — *phobos*. It means *fear, terror, alarm, hush, amazement, or respect*. It usually depicts *a fear that results from a threatening or alarming circumstance*. Great fear came on "all" the church. This word "all" is the Greek word *holos*, which means *the whole, entire, complete* church.

Through all that took place that day, the Early Church received a clear message: *The Holy Spirit who is working inside the church is God, and we need to respect Him and treat Him properly.* The same holds true for us today. The power of the Holy Spirit brings life-giving blessings when respected and handled correctly. But if we mishandle Him — if we lack the reverential fear of the Lord — we will experience negative consequences.

STUDY QUESTIONS

> **Study to shew thyself approved unto God, a workman that needeth not to be ashamed, rightly dividing the word of truth.**
> **— 2 Timothy 2:15**

1. The *fear of the Lord* is an empowering grace that is developed in us by the Spirit of God Himself as we abide in relationship with Him. What does the fear of the Lord look like? Explore these verses from Scripture, and briefly share what the Holy Spirit reveals to you: Deuteronomy 10:12, 13; Proverbs 3:5-8; 8:13; Psalm 34:11-14; and First Samuel 24:14.

2. The Bible is filled with countless promises to you and every believer who walks in the fear of the Lord (*see* Psalm 25:12-14; 112:1-3; Proverbs 10:27; 14:26, 27; 16:6; 19:23; 22:4; Luke 1:50). Take a

moment to look over these passages and identify some of these amazing blessings God has made available to you.

PRACTICAL APPLICATION

> But be ye doers of the word, and not hearers only, deceiving your own selves.
> —James 1:22

1. The fear of the Lord includes a deep awe and wonder for who He is — a trembling that comes from catching a glimpse of His indescribable power and wisdom. Stop and think, *What stirs up this sense of awe, wonder, and trembling inside of me? What aspects of nature, what truths from God's Word, what experiences from my life infuse me with this kind of reverential fear?* Be still for a moment and listen. Then write what comes to mind.

2. In Isaiah 11:1-5, we are given a prophetic picture of Jesus before He made His debut on earth. One of His characteristics mentioned is that He would be filled with and delight in the Spirit of the fear of the Lord. What do you think this means and how might it look in your own life? Take a few minutes to meditate on this passage.

Notes

CLAIM YOUR FREE RESOURCE!

As a way of introducing you further to the teaching ministry of Rick Renner, we would like to send you FREE of charge his teaching, "How To Receive a Miraculous Touch From God" on CD or as an MP3 download.

In His earthly ministry, Jesus commonly healed *all* who were sick of *all* their diseases. In this profound message, learn about the manifold dimensions of Christ's wisdom, goodness, power, and love toward all humanity who came to Him in faith with their needs.

☑ YES, I want to receive Rick Renner's monthly teaching letter!

Simply scan the QR code to claim this resource or go to:
renner.org/claim-your-free-offer

WITH US!

renner.org

facebook.com/rickrenner • facebook.com/rennerdenise
youtube.com/rennerministries • youtube.com/deniserenner
instagram.com/rickrrenner • instagram.com/rennerministries_
instagram.com/rennerdenise

www.ingramcontent.com/pod-product-compliance
Lightning Source LLC
LaVergne TN
LVHW021355080426
835508LV00020B/2291